RIVER ROAD

RIVER ROAD
A MISSISSIPPIAD

ROBERT BENSE

BELLE FONTAINE
EDITIONS

Cover art, *Ribbon I*, by Steve Griffin © 2016, used with permission.

Sketches by Bob Miller © 2016, used with permission.

I acknowledge with gratitude the assistance of Robert Schmidt, Mary Ross, and Taylor Nelson in the journey of this work.

This is a privately published and printed book.
(The figures and narratives herein are purely imaginary, including the voice in the first person.)

ISBN-13: 978-0-9965018-0-4
LCCN: 2016914256

Distributed by Itasca Books

Printed in the United States of America

Belle Fontaine Editions

ALSO BY ROBERT BENSE

Poetry

Readings in Ordinary Time
Listening to the Bowl Crack
Arguments in a Public Space

CONTENTS

Latin Class / xvii

Book One

At Kellogg's Landing / 3

Tongue of the River Speaking / 4

Theophany at Lake Itasca / 8

Crossing between Minneapolis / St. Paul / 10

The Lord Is Enthroned above the Flood / 12

Keeper of the River / 14

Nauvoo Abandoned / 16

Lock and Dam #10 / 17

Plow Breaking Through to / 19

Windows at Tiffany's / 20

Miss Eleanor Runs the Store at Ames / 21

<u>Book</u> <u>Two</u>

Sieur de La Salle / 27

Passages the River Leaves / 29

Monks Mound / 32

Chief Pontiac Enters Mortality at Cahokia / 34

Cherokee Removal / 36

Gypsies at Camp Creek / 38

Elysian Fields of America / 39

Town with a Flat Horizon / 41

Looking for Mark Twain / 42

The "Charlene Thomas" Southbound / 44

Pentecostals at the River Baptizing / 46

Field and Stream / 47

Ringing Ben Katz's Bell / 48

Book Three

The Deciduous Life / 55

Père Marquette at Kaskaskia / 59

Judgment on the Missouri / 61

Lewis and Clark Striking Camp / 63

Piasa Bird / 66

St. Louis: at the Crossroads / 68

Antiphon for Kate Chopin / 71

Running of the Hambletonian / 73

Arsène / 76

Felix Is Dead: an elegy / 78

Staying Close to the Edge / 80

Book Four

What the River Says / 87

River City Longueurs / 92

Treaty of Paris / 94

Ghost Notes / 96

Boxwood / 98

Some Fish to Fry / 99

Retour à Ste. Geneviève . . . / 101

Chester Dreaming / 103

The Big House / 104

December Morning in a Rural Time / 106

Portraits in a Lost Grey / 108

The Burdened Ohio / 110

Mile Zero / 112

Replay / 114

Book Five

Strange Fruit / 121

Time at the Mouth of the Arkansas / 125

Late Morning Prayer in the Arkansas Delta / 128

Delta Oracle / 129

Apotheosis of Elvis / 135

Memphis on the Mind / 138

Echoes from the Red River / 140

Vicksburg / 143

Shiloh / 145

Acorn from Oak Alley Plantation / 147

Folding the Rain on the Delta Queen / 149

Bessie Smith / 152

Delta Wedding / 154

Dusting the Broom: Delta blues / 156

A Modular House Traveling South on Rte. 61 / 157

Shorty Sam's Car Graveyard: an inventory / 159

Book <u>Six</u>

Catching Mass at St. Francisville, LA / 167

Night Voices / 169

Music on the Lower Mississippi: a dirge / 173

Carville / 179

Port Allen / 181

City of Obsequies / 183

Storyville: a sporting life / 186

Coming of the Rain / 188

Returning along the Atchafalaya / 190

At the Sea Mouth / 192

Reading Notes / 193

Acknowledgments / 199

About the author / 201

for my mother and father

I heard the singing of the Mississippi when Abe Lincoln went
down to New Orleans, and I've seen its muddy bosom turn all golden
  in the sunset.

I've known rivers:
Ancient, dusky rivers.

My soul has grown deep like the rivers.

"The Negro Speaks of Rivers"
Langston Hughes
The Collected Poems of
Langston Hughes

Latin Class

Lupercalian February feasts
and Mrs. Styblo lighting
the festal lights for us

though leaning more to
solid republican virtues of drill
and an earlier, sterner Rome

I see her there still
tall in black coat
and broad, black hat

her people stragglers, restless
fresh out of Asia, Troy
led seaward by Aeneas

to Ostia, Bari
nearing the ochre city
as sad Vergilian ghosts

their semi-deponent verbs
she taught by another river
wilder than the Tiber

intrigues of foreign declensions
never overcame our timidity
at once rural, pagan

here, music of the water's purl
began—I tell this to a friend:
the brief songs of those, almost all
now gone.

BOOK ONE

At Kellogg's Landing

The car packed, we start out. Urgencies
boxed. Rufus in the back. There's lightning
to the south. Morning's sacred cows were sent
to slaughter. I no longer advise relatives
on securities. Rural commodities
have been severed from the malice of hard
labor. Horses from hands, the random
from chance. If one could only . . . .

The alluvial landscape we drive through
accumulates particulars. Roadside junkyards.
Children on meth. Women at their windows
wiping tears. Scrutiny peers
from hills sliced by the river we look for.
Behind the wheel I sort out my mind.
The odd comforts. Occasions of want and lack.
Rain seems just. Storm and flood
follow water.

A towboat with barge for eight cars
answers our flashing lights.
We're two passengers but have baggage.
Wind whips up willows on the river bank.
The Mississippi at our heels, we cross over.
Passing horn of a tow, deep sorrowful
out in the current. Water is running high.
There's an attitude in the light rain falling.

Tongue of the River Speaking

What began as vast waves of fire
flows inexorably
toward ice. A river beginning
in tall grasses, headwaters
part northern mist, beyond
stoic ancestors, the journey-work
of time. A short beeline down the flyway
to fading storefront facades, the corseted
embrace of lock and dam.
Bleach bottles, plastic lawn chairs, effluent
of the disposable bobbing to shore. So you say
history is only a story
of things.
              With folded hands Madame Cecile
foretells in her daily column. Princess Shoshanna
in a twangy TV voice decries. Pop celebrities
of spirit joined to commerce, partisans of bile, they
entertain the mornings at our motels.
                                    Ghost winds
and muffled pileus clouds from the melting ice cap
seven hundred miles away. Tamarack headlands
in Paul Bunyan country. Towering roadside statues
of Babe the Blue Ox. Life in large print.
A boy with one leg crops his father's farm.

The courthouse soldier's scattered child.
His baler and twelve cows above the hill
and silo. Bales round as Etruscan columns
grazing angled hillsides. You think
this world is for knowing one afternoon
at a time. And afterward everyone will tell
a different story.
                    At La Crosse a first
encounter with the broad river, onset of black clouds.
A mood. Moods. We were searching
though didn't know it. We turn more self-conscious.
I touch your hair, finger your earrings.
Follow the silver sliver of a jet
toward sunset.
                    We take bridges at Red Wing
and Prairie du Chien. Country roads to nowhere
we had ever been, some brushed by
the beautiful, poisonous, and bitter.
Our fingers and palms anodized
by dewberries in sunburnt fields. At riverbank
mudfish and canoe sidle, slip, and twist by
beneath the flyway's glut, the frenzied
frequencies of low, imped wings. We watch
a robin's mosey, hop, bounce, and tug. It swivels
to watch us.
                    How cordial of Fort Madison
and Keokuk to anticipate
Dubuque. Weathered plywood up to the dentils.
The graffiti-laced lyrics. Failure to survive
photogenic. Where is the camera
to catch these neglected Roman arguments?
An architecture never quite persuasive
in a country of the plain.

Crowded spaces abandoned to open
places. Things—tossed tires, bottles, cans.
The casual ornamenting margins of the local.

                                 A yellow

Caterpillar stalks the edge of Main Street—
dozer blade ravenous. You suspect at once
Bunyan, Babe, and Hels Helsen
have had a hand in this. Over the river
a long, low plume from the nuke plant. Visible
sigh of a nation
                        still at war and accumulating
silences of exhaustion. The undertaker has moved to
Bettendorf. No embalmer needed for death
by attenuation. Death by fire.
By degree and irony. Only death by nodding.
The saloon sandbagged. Everything went in '93.
Again in 2011. Broken levee.
Faith breached.
                The past
is backlit here. A moon from over water
arcs across tower and steeple—bells sold.
The stained glass and marble removed
for franchised pizza parlors. One last time
you look homeward. Remember the public square
schooled in late pagan virtue. And America's Arcadia
morphing into nearby slave lands. The master's lash.
Yes, yes, a garden
early on gone up in weeds.
                        In the river towns
tap tap of the blind man's cane
shuffling behind tomorrow's shadows.
This my patch. Always is the same.
Nothing new. History like calamity.
Always be.

Events mirror revelation
where Nauvoo rises on a bluff above the Mississippi.
Riverbanks of winter nahoo and scrub oak
obscure craft shops, the tidy houses.
Houses of Joseph Smith, Brigham Young.
A great steepled temple rising on the hill
like a statehouse. America raised with Israel
in the sacred annals to exception. There will be
a new set of books. And a lynch mob will murder
prophet and general. A militia berserk with guns
rechannel history. The national faith
now forged.
                    Accounts of the lost patriarch
grown to heroic legend foretell refuge
among the mountains of the West. Stories
now remote from their hard beginnings.
Oxen, mule carts, and wagon trains
will cross the February river. Passable
that year over ice. Handcarts pushed
and pulled through a continent's long winter
for fifteen hundred miles, a *Via Dolorosa*.
Graves of perished Saints on their way to Zion
lie scattered trailside.

THEOPHANY AT LAKE ITASCA

Moon host tinctured in sun's blood
and reed all aquiver. Loon call
settling on the cold. Shoreline
breaking clean and stars invisible.
Suppose, then, this is where
the river begins
and crosses pebbles
that do not cast. A still slim
stream, the narrow waist.
Think of infancy.
Its irrecoverable, slender chronicles.
A waspish navigator
snorkeling across Lake Pepin.
Ospreys on telephone poles
calling ahead to kin
at Pointe à la Hache in Louisiana:
stay, a god is on the way—
genesis of the distant brown fury
now silvering through the birch and larches
and still serene. Already there are
marks of the one true river.
Flattened cans of Bud. Fast food's
polystyrene floating bankside.
Camel butts, catfish, and gars.
Castoffs from ancient works and days.

Afternoons of mosquitoes
harry our passage through scrawny
fields, these acres ungenerous. You think
if not us, who will propitiate
the spirit of the place.

CROSSING BETWEEN
MINNEAPOLIS / ST. PAUL

dusk smelling of traffic   cities serious
with Lutheran   Irish pieties   mills
winding down at star rise

Father Hennepin's street crawling toward
the invisible   northern suburbs edged
with frost   goldfinches gone

—to come here is to have a purpose
we came to be instructed

the river already
plenary
though hiding in a chasm

an unnoticed divinity   unpropitiated
except by poetry   John Berryman
offering serial sacrifice

early on Fort Snelling poised
to tame the West   troops on the horizon
with General Mills at parade rest

on glass silos
stars of a night sea

barrio of steel set in stone
reflecting money   satisfaction
bony children asking for sex   a cigarette

Lipchitz taking ten in the sculpture park
repeating himself
and Oldenburg spoons a cherry

chain link fences   palings   serous membranes
of the Twin Cities   then the small towns of dog bark
river palisades rising up on both sides   roads gritty

this land of breakfasts   latest thinking   mayflies
accordion polkas   evening hours of whiskey sours

somewhere we have passed
where we met ourselves coming
from the northern rectitudes

a tart rancor creeping into our daily—
suspicion   or is it anticipation   that love can fail

THE LORD IS ENTHRONED
ABOVE THE FLOOD

It came down out of the north
mouth pried open wide
kraken or crocodile
the flood upon the waters
a solid front whistling "Dixie"
the vector force and lever
toppling cottonwoods
virgin oak snapped
three, seven, twenty miles outside
its glacial rims
with dervish swirls lashing levees
Valmeyer ghosted
Dubuque, Davenport washed
from their river fronts
Natchez Under-the-Hill savaged

seven years old, I watch
a riverboat paddle among pecan trees
families of Nevois, Laurent, Langlois
waiting on roofs, second-floor porches
their dogs sea-legged in skiffs
soldiers hammering together barges
to rescue livestock, sandbagging
levees against sand boils

the pink, white trash
of a High Plains' summer
washed from Crow Creek, Santee, Williston
now funneled past Caruthersville
the suck of water day and night
and slosh of a maelstrom tail
swept into the sky—
somewhere the tapping of a cane
like the staccato of driven rain
there is lightning in the west.
Another storm approaches.

KEEPER OF THE RIVER

R. E. Lee: Superintendent
of the Mississippi

First winter and spring
of three oblique years:
friends would remember games
of heretic whist and piquet.
French wine, silver, the linen
cloths. Even at Quincy, Galena.

Blood Island engorged.
Port of St. Louis silting.
He came to battle currents
from Alton to Market Street
Wharf. In 1837 barely a captain
in the Corps of Engineers. Success
and failure
waiting in his stars.

                    Sandbar sighting.
Tree snag removal. The river always
at its old tricks. Then the channels
cornered. Sand outfoxed
by his end runs with jetties. Water
beaten with stone. At thirty-one
he feels old. The irksome tasks
of the years here done.

Orders cut. The last ride home.
Virginia still reaching to the Ohio.
A thin line waiting: wife, children
in the scarce shade of cedars.
Slaves to be whipped. A tub of oysters.
Afternoon. The river will slip away.

Nauvoo Abandoned

I could hear no one move. Only fly buzz
and water ripples breaking against shallows
of the beach. I walked through solitary streets.
The town lay under some spell of loneliness
from which I almost feared to wake it.
                                    It had
not slept long. There was no grass growing up
in the paved ways. The carpenter had gone from
his workbench and shavings, his unfinished sash
and casing. Fresh bark was in the tanner's vat.
Fresh-chopped lightwood stood piled against
a baker's oven. The blacksmith's shop was cold.
His coal heap and ladling pool and crooked water
horn were all there, as if he had just gone off
for a holiday.
                I could have supposed the people
hidden in these houses, but doors were unfastened.
I found dead ashes white upon the hearths
and had to tread tiptoe, as if walking down
the aisle of a country church to avoid rousing
irreverent echoes from the naked floors.

paraphrased from the prose of Thomas L. Kane's *The Mormons* (1850)

LOCK AND DAM #10

Below abandoned Nauvoo
its erstwhile aureole now resurrected
by the Saints returning
a liquid crescendo swells to a wave
at the lock and dam.
Cymbal and six muted horns
for two miles of afternoon.
Water music played
as music plays on water—
arpeggios and lowered voice
lock water slowly lifting us
like hills rising to the sky, toward
reflections lake-wide blue at places
windblown willows
bending reeds.
A chorus of clouds over
west bank towns whetted by water
—Guttenberg, Bettendorf.
Sudden sky rumble
and you wonder if thunder
might have pleased the *Meister.*

Everyone gets in line
for the lock
except a no-brainer skiff
with outboard, barges bearing
down, a stern lockmaster
counting bulbous Chris-Crafts
bottom-feeding on sex and beer.
The play stream of the upper river.
On the lower there is nothing
but farming, commerce
diminuendo, whisper.
Like us, you whisper.

Plow Breaking Through to

earth, its palpable resistance
tested
once by horses submitting
to wood and iron.
From a tractor the farmer
precisely lays the furrows
of a spring field. Balm
up from the Gulf
bundled in swelling cumulus
breezes by.
Plowshares silver
cold against slow-turning
loam. Breaking fine, sifting
just at the edge
where the feelings
are. And folding to
the moldboard's steel.
Earth curled
first to nape-blue
of a pigeon's neck.
Then purple-green in the sun.
All hardness of winter
like an attitude held too long
quickly turned from.

WINDOWS AT TIFFANY'S

              Curve of silver
moldboards set in rough iron.
The baler's Farmall red for summer.
Implements angled in shop windows.
John Deere yellow and green
fresh in from meadow and crop.
Oliver's military green—sober
beet-red wheels wound from
crushed garnet. Enameled
prairie golds of Minneapolis-Moline
lacquer smooth and six inches deep.
Racing colors, jeweled hints of
farmers' psyches, inner drives, a bet
on solid iron. You could spend prime
years watching furrows turning purple
over blue. Stubble weave to goldspun
behind Allis-Chalmers orange
combines. You might be drawn by dint
of high seriousness to the grey
melancholy of my uncle's Ford tractor
in Deco-Moderne. Pop-up hood. Seat.
Ferguson hydraulics. Key ignition.
Push starter. State of the art.
But underpowered for the rich obsidian
of river gumbo.

MISS ELEANOR RUNS THE STORE AT AMES

Four long, curving glass cases
their fading rainbow tiers, trays of gumdrops
maple nuts, candy corn

the rationed plenty of a rich land
I once thought this was how
everything was offered

not for sale
and what was wanted
never sold

among tinctures and oils in dry goods
gloves that could have shaken hands
that shook the hand of General Grant

silks thinned to nuance
for insouciant imaginaries once
nodding, curtseying at races and balls

buttons, buttons, buttons
guarding unimaginable tales
with closure and disclosure

aren't we what our memories are

her hand purse-tight with a key—
don't ask me any questions she said
the vitrine slowly unlocking time-dyed cloth

on such extravagant tastes
she would quickly close the case
—so the world was rich like this

having first bent the mind
against all sweets
even licorice

to abet an entire life of wanting
and waiting, secrets
in hiding, ample here, albeit under glass.

BOOK TWO

SIEUR DE LA SALLE

Part voyageur, part feral male.
From Quebec he oared out to sweet water.
Found a river that will run past
toothless hay tedders, rusty horse-drawn
rakes on defaced hillside bluffs, past
disordered childhoods, the lost
poor, happy families in family Fords
and past where the Trail of Tears
crossed over and all are folded
into the river's creases.
                              A continent
nearly to himself, he could hear din
of eagle, crow rise above
the tall grasses. He waited out
standstill days of Algonquin and Iroquois
at war. Watched telltale curls of smoke
break out above the evening
hilltop quiet.
                      After quick decampment
he struck under moonlight for an early
start. His first winter rickracking
a thousand miles across snow and ice.
With shouldered oars and bateaux
on his way to dragoon a wildness
—the Mississippi, an entire continent's
interior life.

On second try he neared
what destiny pulled him toward.
The sea mouth. Cataract and abyss.
But where he reached, the *Meschasipi*
lay slyly hidden four hundred miles to the east
slipped into slow fog of sea shroud.
He is twenty years older now.
Broken, losing his bearing, then his life.

Passages the River Leaves

Mass bells. And Monsignor late winter afternoons
playing Mahler. Solitaire. This was home.
And the road from here to the ferry we've taken often—
our tire tracks left in the river sand's sift.
I know the way from memory. Although you insist
we're lost. *Just what are we making our way*
to? you ask.
            How to answer.
From Cape Girardeau to Anna-Jonesboro
you can look back to clouds
shadowing heavy escarped hills.
There the Cherokee wagons mired
waiting for ferries to take them to scrub
Oklahoma's red dust
                —but I see the lines of your face.
Tears beading at the corner of your eyes.
Asking *can't we go back?*
Meaning home. And the garden you left.
A Christmas tree and candles in the windows.
But there is no home. Only stories
of the nostalgic, and a woman at the window
crying. The river at our elbow draws us
with its sorcery. We travel it repeatedly
to forget the troubles—a sadness
still unclear and only at the edges.

                        You want to know
if this is Herculaneum can Cairo be far?
Here Dred Scot watched from his Thebes courthouse
cell for the paddle boat to take him upriver. You say
where is this pirogue taking us now?
                        Little Egypt
on our left. The Bootheel on the right.
Terminus of the old Gulf near.
The bridge to Sikeston cants at an angle
to the south because this river
cannot be perfected, like all things gathered
to a force and slicing through earth, chert, rock.
The Mound Builders, their galley slaves
flogged—beat back this current
for hundreds of years, hell-bent on reaching Cahokia
in time for a millennium. And then
to disappear, traceless, in the Mississippi
flood.
            You and I go down this road to be.
To have all things validated. Past patches
of Johnson grass. Putt-Putt golf courses.
The dollar stores. Veils of kudzu. Junked-car
lots. We practiced turning down the *grande allée*
to Rosedown like sharecropper children
on a grey afternoon. Pure slumming for us.
Peacocks dragging their fans through rain.
Rain beginning as mist high up in tree moss.
A dog barking at us. Trouble for Rufus, who has
never liked the bruise of argument.
                        Across the road
the billboard in a cotton patch counsels an altar call.
On another, Princess Shoshanna's prosperity message.
Donations accepted.

Rain letting up, we stand
in a grove looking for the photogenic. A rose window
in the west. In the choral hours at sunset
hear a congregation of cicadas at choir
and their arguments by incantation.
Holding fast to bark, freshly risen
after their ascensions, they step out for evensong
from their green bodies, black eyes, the grey antiqued
masks. They require no belief of me.
                                        Again the tapping
of a cane. A voice from the margin
clearing his throat—*history be more
than a story of things.*

Monks Mound

The heartland of the Mississippian Tradition is in the
central Mississippi Valley—northeastern Arkansas,
southeastern Missouri, southern Illinois and western
Tennessee. From here Mississippian ideas radiated
up the rivers as far as the Great Lakes region,
and to the east and west.

Robert Silverberg
Mound Builders of Ancient America

They had a feeling
for the transitory.
Behind a wooden pale
built pyramids and cones.
Yucatán shapes
raised out of dirt
basketed on backs.
They burned their past
past recognition. Sacrificing
the living. Effacing
all effects of elder dead.
Building over, they added to—
or every twenty-four years
renewed their terraces from
ground up. At Cahokia a mound
lifted above all other mounds
its platform for the human and divine
to meet midway.

The Sun Brother
gold leafed, his shell-sequined
arms ruffled in
flyway plumage
spoke to the sky
for everyone else
needing as we do an intercessor
some gesture, sign, succor itself.
He and his cohorts came
from nowhere
anyone ever remembered.
Took duodecimal measure
of the sun between poles
set like masts
on the Mississippi main.
In alluvial bottoms
cultivated corn, maize
raised to the gods
from grains seeded by the sun.
Bartered beads, freshwater shells
for bracelets, burial palls.
For the seashells, they traded pottery
portraying warriors
kneeling to what atrocities.
Red ware for hickory nuts and
sweet acorns.
They left like bees
moving their swarm
for what reason
and to wherever
no one coming after—
Oneonta or Kaskaskia—
could remember.
They wrote nothing in stone, shared
with us a sense
of erasable space, self-
deconstructed, a final event
in the deciduous.

Chief Pontiac Enters Mortality at Cahokia

near the river
at the old French courthouse

plangencies
of an already antique voice
his name remembered
the uncertain details barely

he rode the rivers
until the Illinois and Mississippi
became familiar to him
as the flyways from childhood

his fevered task
the Indian confederacy at risk

with his telling
grace notes falling from his tongue
like bird cries on the wind
a golden hand jabbing the sky

the white man has come to stay

there were early successes
over the British garrisons
—three-quarters of the soldiers
captured, each one massacred

with Odawa, the Ojibwa
he collected scalps, rifles, blankets, horses
—the successes never victories

his people crossing the river west
only outlaw sparrows and an eagle
stay behind with the martyr

tomahawked after British intrigue
his blood soaking the black gumbo
exactly where
never marked

traffic on the nearby Interstate
now heads north to Chicago
through a countryside of Diebenkorn
fields in quondam Firebirds, Bonnevilles

the lank corn green
its silks still thin
when we stop by in early June.

CHEROKEE REMOVAL

The tribe stockaded like prisoners
of war. Soldiers rasping hands
over fire. Cattle and horses
stiffening in the cold. Children
recalled their mothers
crying, men rolling bedding
for the looming trek to Oklahoma.
Soldiers torched houses and barns.
Timbers sparking high in the night
sky. They rode escort to prod
stragglers, thwart escape.
The dying and dead dropped off
in blankets. Ice hung from trees.
The horses lame.
The living will walk, a few ride
more than a thousand miles—
marched to the west's slow beginning
at Green's Ferry on the Mississippi.
A woman who was but a girl then
wrote in a book of remembrances
at Cape Girardeau *I cried*
only once I think. They took
my father. How to forget,
I'm almost the last.

That winter now swallowed
in the hugeness of America
and the blind gut of a river.
A river that remembers nothing.

GYPSIES AT CAMP CREEK

An old woman remembered them
appearing out of the night
before, a caravan stealing in
when she was young
from the secret east
in fire reds, tomato green, final
black. Tethered horses, yellow
wagons ornamented the tawny banks
of the creek. Gypsy women
in layered aprons telling fortunes
her friends were too scared
to believe. Dirty six-year-olds
without toys. Mustachioed men—
tinkers mending thin pots.
Calling themselves Faa's children
they could not recall where
they came from. Would not say
where they were going.
Neighbors lost chickens, a lamb.
Someone among the campers
played a fiddle for hours. A flute.
There was dancing on the dead
leaves from other winters. They left
with the sun for the dangerous
river. Past empty, still fields.
And disappeared into the morning
and morning's dew.

ELYSIAN FIELDS OF AMERICA

No more cows. Outfield's
meadow of blue self-heal
now a cloverleaf
unfolding for an Interstate.
Rapt men in summer
bleachers. In straws, seersucker
suits. Time's polka-dot ties.
Clouded crystal afternoons
liquid with sweat.
My grandfather wheedled
precision out of a dial's
jittery needle and the afternoon's
strung-out voice, the stretched-out
story of a clockless race
run counterclockwise. Cheers
distant, small, forlorn.
The Cardinal's foul, pop flies.
Cincinnati changing pitchers.
The perspective immense
for those who live by moments.
A great green heart
golden from summers past, testing
for steroids and polyester, pulling
at a continent's strings.

Purse of heartland melancholy.
Hum, loneliness of its space.
Mound swagger. Hawk and spit.
Slow descent into time.

Town with a Flat Horizon

It could have risen
like Chartres to success
on recipes for blue and glass.
At the edges, grain
fields lard its hard muscle.
Silos rise up like skyline
towers of a great cathedral.
Three steeples probe for
absolutes. The town's punctual
rhythms, country circadian.
Tomorrow—a mere hiccup—waits
on today. In its late period
this is how time adds up
in the town you come from.

LOOKING FOR MARK TWAIN

Cottonmouths at the water's edge.
Crawfish, earthworms, primal leaf rot.
Little has changed since money
and the judge went south.
Norman Rockwell mugs in antique shops.
On the Missouri hillside
Mark Twain Hotel (boarded up)
Becky Thatcher Diner
HaUCK & Co. Real Estate.
Mannequins explain the milieu:
Tom looking like a young Mormon
Huck fresh out of old money
Jim out of sight.
No auction block
but there is a bale of cotton.
A fake calliope: steamboat a comin'.
We get it—the diorama defying time
in need of dusting.
Looking up, an old lady taking
tickets says to no one
Lord, is it already?
I've mislaid my life.
You ask if Twain ever returned.
I say he did but not to stay
when he had the chance.

Imagine if he came back now
a snakepit investor, bungee-jumping
over the river, perfecter of
winks—eye on the horizon?
Think about it. But you say
you wouldn't have been taken in.

THE "CHARLENE THOMAS" SOUTHBOUND

Copper sky last night, river on fire.
Wheat, corn, coal down.
A tow's fast run with the current
past willow flats. Boys waving.
Bagasse, salt, sulfur up.
Rusted red hoppers, five abreast.
Six in cabled tandem.
Putter and diesel of the diesel tractor.
River world off to bed. Weather reports
rain, turbulence and stall over
the Gulf. Daylong squall.
The captain running on coffee
and cigarettes, his pilot off watch.
Deckhands reading *Playboy   Playgirl*
the Good News Bible. Dancing to
a banjo. Thirty days between shore
leaves. Horseplay grab-ass.
Buoys starboard. Searchlights sweep
silver above the current.
Buffet of water. Fish and drift.
Riverbank poplars, cottonwoods.
Greengrass levees catching
a tournament of white willow flies.
The sky cracking yellow-white. Rain
slamming port windows.

The tow feeling its way. Engine
holding, sudden reverse. Tie-up.
Nylon ropes to saplings. The slow
drizzle. From Cape to Cairo in a day.
To Memphis in two more.
Midsummer night's departure.
Morning steamed up.
Noon opening to blue sky. Biscuits.
Ham and red-eye gravy. Radio chatter
in three o'clock's backyard.
Before bed, a river of fire.
Copper again tonight. Banjo twang.
Dancing. Main deck aft
in the late dark. "Lovesick Blues"   "Cold, Cold
Heart" playing loud below. Silver arcs
search and sweep. Skitter   stare.

Pentecostals
at the River Baptizing

Slough of smooth river silt, their feet
in clayey toehold. Soft warm chill
sucks gowned grown catechumens
down, arms of three deacons
outstretched, secure under
tow of the Paraclete salvaging
from a vast unseen
                    a preacher, deep
to his waist, palms flattened to save—
slip beneath a young man, water
swiping America's slate
clean past Rockwood, a flotsam
smelling of catfish, surplus
and rot
            if seamless soul has a body
aching edged, full-bodied like this
klismos curve of sculpted shoulder
and ass, you have witnessed the Spirit
submit to skin, take on flesh's scrubbed
sigmas of sense seen again
in this morning's renaissance.

FIELD AND STREAM

He is a primal hunter-gatherer.
All his edges male.
Dewberries in July. Squirrel
in season and out. Fishing
until ice. Always alone.
In school he taught us sex.
A shared solitary. Language
not in common manuals.
He knew the nomenclature of
stem and rose. Sessions
of fun, desperate with chance.
The big surprises. At a reunion
I see him walking, slighter than I
remembered, his face still young
with wonder. Hunting, fishing, now
sometimes at night. He doesn't want
to talk about the river's four-knot
compulsions running through
almost everyone's life. Or the hunger
here, the wildernesses inside
torn pockets. Holding back, as if
from dangerous water.

Ringing Ben Katz's Bell

The door to his store announced
entry and exit. At the bell a scrutiny
began—like *An Enquiry Concerning . . .*
His shop outfitted men, though
customers were often women.
Cash-and-Carry. Layaway available.
No one got in or out
without a hand squeezing an arm.
Ben Katz's one eye judged prospects.
The glass eye looked straight ahead.
There were fishing poles. Assorted
guns in popular gauges.
Neat stacks of board-stiff denims
stood starched for toil.
A blue-white smell of sizing
rode the air like riffs of sweat.
Jackets, jeans, overalls
and ready-made suits for boys.
For men ready to marry
and church in winter. For the grave
he carried grey and black.

Though he dressed the farmers
in preferred brown. Collars went
all the way back to celluloid
now yellow. When the Big Box
came to town and nothing sold
Ben Katz packed up, closed the store
and slipped away. They say a collector
from Maine now has the door.

BOOK THREE

The Deciduous Life

These are restless times for us. Searching for
something undefined, we look for landscapes
that might calm. The dark wood still lay off the map
of our wandering, something we half-knew. A broken
hearth and childless—we are drawn back
to where the green blade rises. Both of us to start over
and make old narratives new. But everyone knows
no two stories are ever the same.
                                        We watch
fat fields of legumes sweep by, rubbing lazily
against levees. Around Three Forks, country people
still in families, families still together
sitting sprawl-legged on front yard benches
shelling peas. The brown yard swept. A rooster
and two pigs at their feet. Grandchildren
tying the cat's tail to a stick. Ding-ding—
a five-year-old tugs his make-believe steamboat
to a front porch landing. Two rivers nearby.
In confluences for the evening, their reeds playing
at night river juju. In the yards, katydid karaoke
above the dark's soft hush.

Crotch of the continent:
fish-fetid, humid. Bite of acrid fumes. Industrial
bile. From the navel of Memphis on the hill
to here. At the seven-mile crossroad
Robert Johnson meeting the Adversary
picked up his guitar. In August languor, in torrid
nights the men, quick, take their women.
And the women broaden and beam to receive their
men, bear bold children.
Taste of salt, sea smell of river gism.
Of jazz. Ma Rainey leaning on the mahogany.
Gold-toothed. Diamond studs.
Rattle of glasses.
Above the green belly of a fat
continent it's always leaf and unleaf. And relief.
The white cane's rhythm you hear
beating against the temporals of your skull
is the drumbeat of retreat—
what if
after coming this far there be nothing
after coming this far?
We have reached the epicenter
of eighteen-wheelers. North lane/south lane
antiphonals. Scott Field fighter jet synodals.
In the long ruin of the poor
abundance runs up its flag. Spoiled
porches, broken roofs. Baby blue Buicks
jacked up on stove wood. Used tires
for resale. Butylenes retreaded, resold at Cairo.
The Nash Rambler on loan to memory
and where the red barn stood at Chester
sorghum follows a field. We lag behind on the way
to becoming what our memories are.

An ordinary
nexus now snakes the continent with four million
American miles of corridor. Some we follow.
A journey taking its edges from
Johnson grass, junkyards. Litter.
The detritus of old Federal liberties.
Bear
and cougar have been driven to the hills with the wild
blackberries. Along with meadow roses, Choctaw
and Chickasaw leave diminished. Shawnee
and Michigami absorbed into the diaspora of lost
tribes, lost kin. Whites and Blacks have this place
all to themselves. With possums
and persimmons. Redbone hounds.
Don't hold your breath. The family
of man is in a mood. The river current
sucks sourly at the levees. Tow and barges
churn through mornings and afternoons.
Cargo braced, lashed, passing America's
high plain of war. Vicksburg
on the bluffs. Cottonmouths flail in a slough
water's slurry.
Princess Shoshanna says she reads
Ayn Rand Sundays at breakfast while spreading sorghum
on her boudin. Madame Cecile stays in touch
with volatile spirits embedded in new encryptions
fresh from the East.
There are days in August when
I want to become fluffy white and imperial. Slink past
the sinister House of Neptune.
Far from the haze of puts and calls. Stale
office coffee. The wheeze of bonds. Sailfloat
from Algiers to Venice. Over
Port Sulphur.

Over Empire.
Where big hulls anchor, five decks
below the levee, five decks above
and boys with BB guns dead aim
at cockroaches and bumblebees.
And everyone gets cancer
for Christmas.
        Quincy to Hannibal
the sweet gum and sumac
turning to fall. A half-submerged log
floating downriver like an alligator
below Alton's bluffs. There Père Marquette's
eye caught the cliff-painted Piasa Bird
fluttering from wounded sleep
at the gate to Little Egypt. Rufus, locked in
the car, barks at birds in the birdless air.
All his life he has feared eagles, terror birds
and things that might drop from the sky.
You say what lies ahead looks
suspiciously like an end, serene and pure
unornamented and polished.
Licked clean by worms.
        Well, this is preparatory.
Yes, say it—purgatorial. And brooding errands
still call us to the wilderness.

Père Marquette at Kaskaskia

Illini hyperbole.
Whirlwinds writhing just inches
above earth.
Tornadoes coloring air
iridescent. The miraculous
disguised as ordinary
protocol.

With Jolliet, Marquette had gone as far
as Spain and the river allowed
if you were French.
Claiming and reclaiming
the river valley for France.
Its flora, fauna, the aborigines.

Here he had nearly finished his slow
farewell to body. The Illini.
Turning from breviary to an Easter
morning crisp, and remembered
in his diary, he touched gently
what had touched him hard.

Spring winging in on the breeze, tall
grasses running to the soft river lips.
The water cold from
High Plains winter—in a fertile
southern village of Illini
he planted a naked cross
alongside the maize.

Native eyes now eager for news
from elsewhere
watched for tidings
black robes bore. And faces that never knew
the whip of *no*
asked for his report from beyond
the mute, vaulted sky.

They wanted importuning
litanies. Ceremonies
of salvation. Incense.
Self-sufficiency of Illinois abundance
sloughs full of fish
fowl and cultivated corns
no longer enough.

JUDGMENT ON THE MISSOURI

Crazy Horse on a hill
hand to brow:
Oglala battles won, the long war lost.
Bluffs close to a silver horizon
burning with morning's alloy
tarnished now in sunlight.
We argue about everything.
Directions. How to park the car.
Stand at opposite ends
on a barge, its cargo of growing poison
between us like the balanced equation
of a canoe.
The Missouri
doglegging through Indian lands
since Pleistocene spring.
From the Great Divide
past sand hills, flint hills.
Witness to our arguments.
Bringing sharp counsel to
hunters, trappers, traders.
The Indians and soldiers.
Lewis and Clark.
Offering everything to beguile.
Most of a farm. A Norway spruce.

Coffins from a burial ground.
At the brown edge, water dividing
four ways in the long course from Eden
and River Brethren dunking
in their white robes, standing afterward
before our Lord unstained.
Voices of a worshipful company
praising: what would Easter be
without the Pentecost?
After unremarked woe—droughts, locusts, flood
further customary gifts
remain to be withdrawn, one by one.
All that is left is a feeling born of spare and lean.
Nature's cold calculations when added up.
The animal in us is adequate
for now. We use it
to touch everything
blinding us as we move apart.
You say nothing lasts forever.
And so it doesn't.
But then what are we still looking for?
White sweetnesses of limestone
lie ahead, and clear water of arterial creeks.
Sour tang of Osage oranges.
Morning's pink light in the east.
General Custer's blood on the horizon.
And weather grumbles out of the badlands.

LEWIS AND CLARK STRIKING CAMP

The Corps of Discovery settled that winter
under cottonwoods on River Dubois. Off
Highway 3, a road sauntering through the backwaters
of my childhood. They were watchers of
continental weathers, and the Mississippi
was soon frozen. The Wood River solid.

We hunt up and down for relics. Find only
wind in the cottonwoods. A Corps past discovery.
Fossils, arrowheads and mastodon skeletons
surrendered to the rivers. Ashes of encampment
washed to wherever by shifting channels.

Clark drilled his Kentucky marksmen
like an army. All winter, corpsmen
stir-crazy, in whiskey fights
bringing Indian women into camp.
Trouble would follow
the entire trail.

There was work to do.
Reading the Missouri, its legends.
Rounding up guides—the French traders, trappers.
In St. Louis provisioning
for the keelboat:

> 3,400 lbs. of flour
> 750 lbs. of salt
> 300 lbs. of tobacco.

With early spring you still can hear rifle cracks
of river ice splitting. Roar of the Missouri
a mile away wrestling the Mississippi
for bed space. Above the sloughs, watch tall egrets
return. The poetry of blue herons.
Congresses of water moccasins.
Lewis will take his Newfoundland, Seaman.
Clark, his slave, York—with him
from childhood.

They found 178 new plants, 122 animals.
A badger, skinned and stuffed
will be sent to President Jefferson.
Private Pierre Cruzatte fiddled
schottisches and reels to astonish
Indians. And remember home.

On the Missouri they met their first
bison herds, short-grass prairies. Decimated
Mandan villages. The Rockies. A rendezvous
with Salish, Sioux, the Nez Percé.
Violence of winter ratcheting, they had to eat
some of their horses.

Sacagawea saw them to the sea.
The party will go eight thousand miles.
Crossing the continent to take a year longer
than expected. And by then
the West will have moved.

PIASA BIRD

it tormented the Illini, carried
off braves until a final volley
of arrows entered its furious breast
Local Legend

You want to see the painted
dragon bird above Grafton
I think it's a reproduction
you say *aren't we all*

we drive down the Great River Road
from Quincy, looking out
for anything green
and low flying
—forewarned and prepared
our telephotos in the back
of the Cherokee wagon with Rufus
fidgeting, nervous

it was shitting on cars
barreling down Highway 3
all afternoon—
sand truck and State Police
alerted

there it is
well, bigger than life
in Père Marquette's journals . . .
two painted monsters
which at first made us afeard

a deer with red eyes, a tiger's beard
something of a man's face
a body covered with scales
and its tail winding about the body
in red, black, green

think of the indolence
of blackbirds
then glimpse the solitary monster
and watch it nesting
on the bluff, body in profile

posing for the long life of legend
and after bird whistle, clank, clatter
of scales
the slow flutter of miscellaneous
phantom feathers

one day you'll look up
it will have fled again
a bird with an epic song to sing
and we'll be gone.

St. Louis: at the Crossroads

Falling from government of the east
the west begins here. The south reaching
just this far: a meeting of waters
after ceremonies of mating serpents at Grafton.
At Alton. St. Louis. Mid-journey, we are close
to home again.

A god in brown
swirling past, naked to the continent.

The city once outfitter to the frontier.
Greatness seemed possible.
History had a direction
and it was headed here.

In 1904 everything was. A World's Fair.
Train tracks of the nation passing across
the arching new bridge in love with its river.

Commerce of malt, leather volatiles
accompany the slow descent of Broadway.
Summer's mercy lodging in the shelter
of clouds. Hawserless, huge boat
rings still fasten to the cobbled landing.

The botanical garden rising on Shaw.
Boxwood perfume and billow follow.
African violets, the Jewel Box anticipate
Bucky Fuller's geodesic rainforest.

Field songs move upriver
in the dank darkness of riverfront bars.
Turn into a deep jazz on the way to Kansas City.
Chicago. Mr. Handy has been through.
Galvanized pails of summer beer
quaffed on marble stoops.

After a draft or two
the poets leave.

Private retreats stand guard on gated streets. Only frost
at dawn and autumn smoke violate their inner sanctums.
Certainly nothing too new.

But against the odds, art corners the market
for Max Beckmann in River City.
Museum rooms that cool the summer
line up with cartoonish
bourgeois demeanors. Misdemeanors.

Louis Sullivan's terra-cotta leaves
curl at decorous edges of the Wainwright Building.
Other vine leaves are wrought in iron agony.
Along the streets' transparent fragility
old glass lies shattered. Plywood shuttering
windows that once gazed out
on the West's deep frontier.

For fifty years trains backed
slowly in, pulled slowly out of the train shed
until they found it too much trouble.

And the American League moved its game
east. The Browns learning to fly like Orioles.

Seidel trucks in blue and gold. Deliveries of coal.
Summer ice before the sidewalk drip
of rusted air conditioners jutting through transoms.

Opera in the park. Bowling and lotto.
Pinochle. Deep animal fear
of the serious. The trains are gone.

No one who wants to go is left.

Antiphon for Kate Chopin

A survivor, the frame house imperfectly shared
    on Magazine Street, her memories pared back
        for a reliquary to be carried from New Orleans

a flat outer world tipping to ennui, scenes
    of meddling priest and cacique
        and the black moods of Cajun country, then

nights like nocturnes, pelican and loon
    following, and two weeks on water at peace
        steamboat boiler whisper, paddle chop

threading her past to the past, a last trip
    between antipodes—New Orleans and St. Louis
        her chamfered borders, each with a token

civility, and taking what could be taken
    books, children, the broken template of happiness
        porcelain bowls and a mirror

with the bridal beauty of this world behind her
    the black Louisiana green
        and a portmanteau of accumulated liaisons

having their uses, stain of the river and its seasons
    running down the back of her stories unseen
        like a shiver

love's high-strung lute put away elsewhere
    with the ferment of rising yeast
        the salons, shelter to times remembered

and evenings of contested ember and ash
    powers knowing no peace
        find an address in St. Louis.

RUNNING OF THE HAMBLETONIAN

Mares snorting on the magma
of sunrise. Nostrils flush with
fence tops. A nibble from the fancywork
of curling willow leaves
late summer dry. Dusty roads
racing levees, north to south.

At the country fairs reckless reveries.
And a feeling you have—the certain
lightness of winning.

These races run since a giddy Scamander
cut through the Trojan Plain
all the way to Du Quoin
a special mark stands out

you can't miss it—
a turning post
in a now-forgotten game
where the outward course turns home

home ribboned in crepe paper here
red, blues, and Coca-Cola underwriting
the hoopla. Flatt and Scruggs warming up
the stands. Fury of leather and scratch.
Run, Mollie, Run.

Greyhound. Pronto Don.
Adios. Hambletonian, his honor
forerunners lost to background
the long memory of stud books and Pegasus—
Kanthaka and Burak newly put to harness.

Horses learning their Aesop
from a long narrative line.
The sport
barely past this side
of bloodshed.

Nine hundred pounds of equine
lightness then
straightening the spine-curved earth.
Yet so little to bet on.

Heat-baked clay breaking into
tiny puffs of dust.
The trot:
right front. Left rear.
Left front. Right rear.

The sulkies racing just behind, scarcely
earthbound. Leather buggies
—war chariots, really
lifting from midsummer afternoon
and its flat tones of gravity.

Bettors
glad-handing fate, putting down a wager
on beauty, hunch, a guess.

The records of course, of course.
But dreams spreading across
spreadsheets, winning spreadsheets
coming up short. Except one.

In sport all else is losing.
And winning and losing here
was the hard work of arriving
before anybody else.
Though in a calculus of the timeless
everything comes out even. Almost.

ARSÈNE

hours on flitting wings, weather permitting
sitting on the Creole porch, his feet on the rail

and yet time and wait, whistling at the dark
a witness to what time forgets
ancestors, heirs now passing by

but who has time to breathe

fog out at the river
trailing river musk
a tow's bullfrog croaks

searching for stories shaped by their rumors
stories you know told over and over
rhythms never straying from the local familiar

twins at the Duclos'

Mrs. Palmer at church
Monsignor pampered by
parish wives and women

day and night, the seasons in their shadows
caught in his chair's quarter-tilt

who has time to breathe

visiting sharecropper farms, sidekicking with
Emile, the county *patron*
lunch at Petrie's where everything comes out

old Perrot has killed himself again

the night treble
of cottonwoods in the yard, the high sorrowful
of the saddest hour

now Rosemarie's tight with the priest
that's for sure

news travels fast
a bell tolling for someone
you know, who knew you

who has time to breathe

FELIX IS DEAD: AN ELEGY

His room stands next to the tracks
shutters closed
it's six a.m.—what on earth?

I saw him smile only once—
the bodhisattva public face
his limping leg

getting the *patron's* lunch
cleaning cesspools, taking the heat
at white people's barbecues

descendant of forbears brought upriver
auctioned to a Chouteau
you do what you have to do

wife dead, pew kept
their fled children living in diasporas
away from the cross of here

alone his last night
what could he have heard
above the shrills, shrieks of urgent trains

a blackened trunk, strap hinges
powdery from waiting, packed to go
cold ashes in a cold stove

heavy dew on the night grass—
one will wonder how hard it is, limping
into sleep, shuffling into the future past.

Staying Close to the Edge

The Kaskaskia, a tributary, heading south
from Carlyle under a quarter moon
makes straight for the muddied river.
Called the Okaw here, a narrow channel
for uncollected griefs.
Fishing skiffs netting carp and perch
for sale in Chicago. Men posed in leather
their bodies pricked and stung
by the catfish they catch.
This trip has packed conundrums.
Endless questioning, musings—
how can you be happy when I am not—
we're always running from the crazy
with a hamper of hurt—though to be sure
our accounts differ.
I recall what we once were.
Mornings of your smiles.
Smell of the warm, fresh from love.
Your jokes. The psychiatrist and the bulb—
we are what our memories are.
And come as close as we ever did
to what it was we were looking for.
But our centers have shifted
from fixed, common places, their stories.

At riverbank, our skin offers
no barrier to burdock, the reeds, slicing
Johnson grass. Or our eyes
to each other's bristle.
Then how to restart yet again.
We trace our futures at a beery bar.
Draw circles with our fingers
in the glasses' sweat. Sit near the door
as if a private garden of balm
hid somewhere near. Our fingers crossed.

BOOK FOUR

What the River Says

You want to know who settled here.
What is authentic.
After 400,000 years
of thrust and rush through Bemidji, past Rock Island—
banks and bluffs stripped to erode another day
the maples, oaks cut for steamboat boilers.
Time's dialectic sweeping away the fixed banksides
of a glimmering, nervous basilisk with an appetite
for travel. Madame Cecile stays the hand of
destiny in the morning paper, reaching into time's vast
miles for the last glacier leaving its predatory weep.
(Look for it behind the moraine. A hill, still damp
on the long prairie, hiding red, orange, green
stones the Tuscarora traded in.) She reads
palms and horoscopes on the side.
Offers delphic pericopes
to the eagerly innocent.
                           Princess Shoshanna
eyes real estate. A keen observer of the nation's
morals on radio, TV. They are one person
but two personas.
                           And she keeps a fire at all times.
Unties four knots in a scarf. The griot, a shaman
cutting in the sugarcane outback
won't return before dark.

In lone lament of a candle
he will take from his grimoire
a pony of whiskey
thimble of powdered sugar
and a tablespoon of molasses.
The future and time's pluperfect
are filtered through a handkerchief
soaked in turpentine. The recipe
kept in the pocket of a ritual doll. But available
after the show. Or send
twenty dollars now.

>   *Death like poisons*
>   *swim with the alligators*, a voice says.
>   *If you a hardhearted man*
>   *wintertime's comin'. A long life*
>   *be wasted. Sins is the root of this.*

He hobbles behind a white cane.
Wears his blindness like a badge.
Princess Shoshanna turns, and says
I saw you cutting the clouds from Paphos.
All the way to St. Louis.

>   Eagles above Grafton

know these fields. Day and night
sibilance and tintinnabulation of wings.
Insects ten times older than the river.
Crawfish frass, their silken holes
slip-plastered to glass, caked with clay.
After boarding the IC Line
at the Port of New Orleans, settlers looked for
whatever looked like home. Home will take some
getting used to.

>   Nothing from Hickman to

Portage des Sioux looks quite like any place else.
Like Lower Saxony. The Ring of Kerry.
Potato fields of Poland. In rural exiles
women stand at their windows crying.
We are what our memories are.

You can see there never will be any settling down
in this land. Princess Shoshanna says
nothing agreed on stays fixed or standing—who knows
whether the Army Corps will even keep their
channel nine feet deep.
                              You can hear time's
long unravel here. Old men waving from porches, their
slow talk of beginnings. The end. Of burial mounds
like hills. Along a white-dust road they carry fishing
poles. Chicken liver bait. Catches of catfish, bluegills.
Some limping. They spit in old coffee cans. Denizens
of a remote republic closer to an end than any beginning.
String-belted citizens. You embrace one.
Your grandfather's grandfather. Spittle
at the corner of his mouth, his shoes
untied. You're astonished at the ceremony
of dry death.
                  Buzzards swoop low.
On becalmed days you can hear yourself
think about the lengthening notes
of purling silence. A natural music attracting
Crockett, Daniel Boone. Boone's short
Quaker peace replacing frontier blades.
And the arc of Lincoln punt-paddling a flatboat
west, past the pirate caves. Slap-slap and piddle
of the dipping oar for weeks on end.
At Cairo, turning the corner, sweating
into the mainstream. There, Samuel Clemens
snagged a sandbar. And Dickens took
America's fever. Flood of the sweet past gainsaid
and hanging in the trees like aftermath.

                                        A bouquet
of whiskey air, the lye of wet ashes—
wind blowing east. And rise of purple smoke
plumes. A sour mash still crouching in the brush.
Over wide Ozark woods, secrets brood. Pot farms.
Tall plants like post oak saplings. New kitchen
meth labs in lean-to cabins. In trailers under a tree.
Explosions. Women at their windows crying.
Burnt over hillsides. Bile of acrid smoke.
Men packing heat at 7-Eleven.
Under metal porches good old boys drinking
mash water. White lightning, rye.
Shades of bye-bye Miss American Pie.
Solitude's *longue durée*, the afternoons
whittling down a slow proposition.
Driving the Chevy to the levee past barnsides
of Red Man's fading green and red.
Chewing their tobacco.
Watching the flood rising.
                          Iron bedstead and cornshuck
mattress. Canned heat. Smoky jook below, sandbagged.
Great tongues of fire trimming the wick
of an idol's lamp. High volatiles
of kerosene and petroleum jelly.
                          Grey smoke puffs.
Incantory whorls . . . <u>oh</u> my God . . . clamp your chomps
on this stick of tea . . . oh <u>my</u> God . . .
the jivey smoke of Waters . . . come on baby
now get high with me . . . oh my <u>God</u>.
Coke. Whiskey in a tin cup. Blood.
Bloody Island. Return of pain's wide
amplitude. And a voice
if it's like what it's usually been bein'
it won't be any too good.

On the motel TV
I surf for scores, the closings, news.
Princess Shoshanna is saying
I have molasses and cream for breakfast.
Smothered chicken for supper. Plenty of greens.
The switchboard lights up. Tens of thousands
of her fans calling in for recipes.
And when I see a tree, she says
I think of an ax.
            The bridge to Chester
up to its chin in water again. Kaskaskia under.
You once looked at the map and said this island
is stolen. The levee at Pujol hasn't held.
Prairie du Rocher gets by. Barely.
Phillipetown long gone. Citizens practice
losing to the slow tap of a cane. In sleep
they practice ruin.
Who would ever want to stay?
To come back? you ask me.
One has to wonder. Once you had liked it here.
This is where your roses grow.
And Rufus the Airedale hunts
his bones. Ready. Standing by the door.
Waiting.
            We sit in another sour, dim bar
dodging each other's barbs. A ceiling fan ticking.
Fried catfish. Pickled eggs beet-red in a jar.
TV banter. Whiff of the river. From the jukebox
string-twangs of Mother Maybelle's autoharp
and "I Told Them What You're Fighting for."
Unknown to us then
we would never come back.

RIVER CITY LONGUEURS

Frankie's from Kansas City
Johnny from Joplin
they hook up on Gravois in St. Louis

that's fateful Clotho packing it in:
it's not six a.m. but her work is done
if her work is ever done

Johnny flashes diamonds and gold
Frankie knows only what her mother said

there's no good to men

Lachesis darts into 323 S. Grand
to beat the heat: to ravel or unravel...

a woman needs two things
a man has only one to give

there's a lot to do, she's the first to say
her work is never done

Johnny likes his honey
there's always enough to go 'round

well yes and no: there will be no woman
in Leland, that Nellie Bly in Memphis

a man has only one thing to give

too simple but true
Lachesis says to no one in particular

Frankie sees Johnny has done her wrong
she says this ain't right to Johnny's .44

there's been some mistake
—this weaver's art is not a science

that Broadway river bar no place to be
Frankie does a rooty-toot-toot on Johnny

already the choral section rehearses:
implacable Atropos sings with her scissors

Johnny has three holes in him now
and Frankie's in the jailhouse too

Lachesis knows which skeins color
justice black, white, impartial

half of River City says love's like that

the threesome fold their hands in their laps
waiting to repeat their thankless work

Frankie's from Kansas City, Johnny from Joplin
—that Stetson hat on the stool? Uh, oh—
here comes Stagolee, a cruel man.

TREATY OF PARIS

A plague of locusts
at Prairie du Rocher.
Armyworms crawling on everything.
Like 1763, two floods in one spring.
In the middle of summer
the present eternal:
les anglais are coming
cohorts already in the hills.
At Chafflin Bridge, Belle Fontaine.
The priest at Ste. Anne prophesies
*le jour viendra quand tout le monde
parlera anglais.* Even baptism
will be in English.
The Fort Chartres commandant
practices raising marigolds
after lowering the lilies of France.
His garrison marines demand
tobacco, lighter leggings.
The pentagonal silhouette of the fort
shadowboxes with a river
that has removed itself by a mile.
Forgotten by France, by everybody.

Today, levees higher than
the battlements.
Out there—
there's nothing but mosquitoes
for company, Mrs. Duclos says
at the diner.
I pay the check, take a toothpick.
Well you go for the history, I say.
Tell the truth, she says, *that's something*
I could do without.

Ghost Notes

That hum in the humid river air—
mosquitoes on the way to food
now checking out the constants of our schedules.
The arachnids entangling us in web.
Dust mites cleaning up after our decay.
Silverfish traveling in our luggage—
with us do Rome in a day. With the arthropods
the pyramids tomorrow.
                                    Exoskeletons
—two steps away from grass—find the river
floodplain and digress into wood, woolens.
Have ancestors like us. Skeletons
hidden in embarrassing closets.
With the trilobites the fossils
of crustaceans and millipedes
provide a narrative to the past's dead ends.
And like us aspire to rise above
origins. With song and dance
beetles put on floor shows of current chic.
Early painters of the Apocalypse
lepidoptera hint at spontaneous rapture.
The luna moth, sucked into morning
outside a kitchen door, joins the saved. While
an outing of Pavons lingers, batting
above Bayou Lafourche.

                         This land barely
warmed from its long, semi-liquid sleep
and earth already turning blue-bug green.
The future, a beetle wing-beat behind retreating
glaciers. Skies under weight of constant
metamorphoses. Mississippi air fecund
with gendered permutations.
What more can you say about the insect world
fretting its own nervous buzz.
Like proto-rock and R&B, engorging on overload
these polymaths in concert, their pop details
requiring only one or two notes.

Boxwood

for Laura Melliere Moehrs

Her drive turns and doubles back
round an island "O" of boxwood.
Darting between shadows and light
guinea hens scratch in the gravel
for chafers and night crawlers.
In the blue overhead
swirls of kitchen smoke.
Yard caladiums bend from chill.
Leaves drifting under catalpas and ash.
Her ancestors carried rooted cuttings
of box to wherever they settled
leaving clouds of green
somnolent in the river's languid air.
For thirty miles, in directions known to
her, where houses stood
or next to foundations of fallen-in
barns, ravaged billows of evergreen
once buttoned to now axed earth
and to something going. Almost gone.

Some Fish to Fry

Five squat shacks in decline
across the tracks where
a leaning school gathered
them, people of color—
très noir even for the French
who named them
Arnaud, Hippolyte.
Surnamed them into families
Micheaux and Boudreaux.
And in town allowed
three black pews.

Grace is the rent
when needed. So redemptive
grace requires leaning into
canebrake swaths, sweating
and July field hollers, machete
cuts. Survival, hell and penitential.
They never had the money
for the things that cost money.

Forebears, kin—all that is
left at Prairie du Rocher
discarded in the one corner
a cemetery wedge permitted.
With a frowning priest at the lip
of the grave, on such occasions
standing in for Jesus.
Slippery gumbo dirt
in this bottomless land
feigning a cultivated end.
Stake and blood-dark claim
now disputed. Earth was no friend.

Seigneur
ayez pitié de nous

RETOUR À STE. GENEVIÈVE...

Limestone, cast-iron gratings, scarred facades.
French, deceptive and fronting for former wealth.
The riverfront is lost. Refuge once from English
rule, a town now satisfied with impersonations.
Its tissue shrunken by flood. The few trees
haggard with summer burn. High on a single hill
the huge church shades a treeless square.
Roses, mint, and basil mingle in formal and informal
alliances. Tourist edifices the town's newfound
faith. Empty Creole houses set inside
kitchen and ornamental gardens
bared to vertical board and beam
for our belief. You invite me
to the Old Brick Hotel
for clabber milk pie, coffee.
The way up on our walk, heavy and silent.
Our lives no longer aligned, the coffee cups
fill with languors. In the tiny museum
you first feel the wistful architecture
of afternoons, their long descent
into elegy here: Vivaldi's *Seasons* coming from
an armoire, boxed coiffeurs from other times
yellowed muslin, silks faded into fragment.

You think everything dies with us
and usually before. Especially these gardens
in country parterres with clouds of boxwood.
The sad scent of summer shadows reminding us
of us, their shapes scissored to a formal absence.

CHESTER DREAMING

The town has given away much
to keep up with time.
Greek Revival courthouse. Small
hotels. The riverboat landing
now plowed by train tracks.
A lone tree withering at the branches
next to a single bench. Old men sit
knob-cheeked and dentureless, smoking.
Old money from milling winter wheat
settled in bluff-top mansions
their windows catching the orange
arterials of a late December sunset.
Matters unknown to me in childhood
the cold unrest of its empty streets
its eviscerated heart
my mother in her solitude dying here.
Popeye, a native, long gone to
hyperbole, brought back in brass—a fit
of memory standing at the edge of town
and his swagger a presence again.
The town's upturned collar
warding off the past and future.
Easy to wonder what audacious dream
passed through in haste.

THE BIG HOUSE

There was no grand manor, only tarpaper
shacks and ten thousand acres of hill clay and buck-
shot farms scrabbled across two counties

taking from the earth—
Emile took what could be got easy
and the price was always right

his house a shed peeling white
on a back street, his court held there
Sunday mornings for his tenants

needing a cow, $300 for hernia repair
when to sow alfalfa, or my father
wanting to let a field go fallow

sharecropper wives and kids stacked outside
in hammered pickups, waiting while he wrote
everything down in a ledger

Emile seemed bemused by his feckless
renters: like a talk show host
he insisted on the stories of throwaway lives

the last time I saw him
they'd replumbed his aorta in Memphis
with polyvinyl tubing

back home again, nothing working well
in his head, sequences misfiring
mind shutting down

thinking he had helped those
down on their luck
and those who would never get up without help

in his own house he couldn't walk
with cane or walker, feeling like
shit he said

the grey cloth ledger out of sight
he wheezes, coughing, hawking
—he knows they did something in Memphis.

December Morning in a Rural Time

He rose like others in the four o'clock
blue-black to slaughter hogs. The sky still
pricked by pinhole stars, as if to obscure
further the darkness he was charged with.

Tall flames swathed steaming water
in cauldrons. From the shadows men
moved toward kettles. And dawn began
to reveal the day's guile.

Quick, close-range reports
of a neighbor's .22—squeals softening to
whistle, silence. A shame he felt like guilt.
Then thump of dead weight.

Carcasses dangling from tree limbs
over water for scalding. *Pling* of bell scrapers.
Bodies splayed, opened like diptychs.
At the edge dogs snapping for tossed offal.

Fat tissue peeled off like onion silk.
Innards of two-hundred-pound animals gutted
into tubs. A peritoneal stench the revenge.
Someone skimming boiled kidneys to eat.

Racks of sausage extruded from a black
cast-iron press. Klumpenwurst to be eaten
quickly. Bacon, hams will take months to cure.
Snow will fall long before.

No longer squealing for their lives
the hogs have become known by their parts.
He, especially, had almost loved them
and knew them by their names.

PORTRAITS IN A LOST GREY

Theirs, one of the last I saw
    a cabin staked to a hillside
        porch pulling away

two corrugated sheets
    from the rusted roof
        in a gully below

Dorie, George's wife, never feeling
    quite right in her head
        after a childhood fall

wash lines with no run
    up and down the hill   squirrel
        for dinner, supper

he was a tenant farmer
    like my father up-creek
        night hunting together

possum, raccoon, skunk
    the virgin woods sour
        with black oak

his twelve dogs ate chickens
    wouldn't hunt
        days he ran traps

farmed with mules
    didn't trust horse sense
        the iron of tractors

he said the only pain
    he ever felt was in his
        dick   they had no children

when he died, *when*
    isn't clear, Dorie
        no longer could notice

when she died, no one
    was *sure*   she wasn't one to leave
        with a fuss and a chicken in the pot

they've been gone so long
    I'd like to see them again   George
        whistling "Jimmy Crack Corn"

in the quick light of a clearing
    Dorie hanging to the porch rail
        calling George to squirrel.

THE BURDENED OHIO

Beauty creviced between earth
and sky. Worn green hills. Mysteries
of unexpiated greed from behind the stark
iconostasis of gutted Appalachia.
The subject here: a lesser theogony:
three rivers on the way to one
from Pittsburgh on.

Tributary? Unitary? A river falling out
of the east like an unexpected guest.
Worn but majestic
against hard brick edges
of unforgiving river towns that remember
wrongs, drift of neglect.
One year the mayor left with girl and till.
A sordid affair in the Methodist choir.
Local rumors looking for a landing
before going under at the Cairo merge

where the Ohio takes a ninety-degree turn.
Or as gossip waiting at the Gulf for
—for the national news that makes it that far.
Along the way the river washes
part of the American screed
clean of its excesses. To remind us
of America's story, unconfined by history.

Will you, water godhead from our past
buoy, wash us all
back to shore in time?
There at the big bend, with its locust
hum, a new river furrowing the continent's moist
belly, clouds wet and low. The past
now disguised as undertow.

Mile Zero

A diminishing point, the river's mileage
markers starting twice—once on the river
at Cairo like a mood washing over
and again at the Passes
like an accounting about to commence

at the upper zero
promise of a place where
a black man's freedom might begin
forty acres—or five
a mule to come later
or none of the above and never

south from the same mark
the river turns needy
for special grooming by the Army Corps
you can see from maps its run
bound by Paleozoic logic
once the river sets a course
and feels its profligate way with gravity

we went as far as we could go
a parting
as indistinct as water dividing
I remember the voice, your high laugh
low clouds like waves
and clouds that darkened your days
now days of silence on the river
and the years erasing what I remember

rear-ending cumulus hang over the Gulf
the lower marker lost in sea grasses
at the upper, brass-green clouds
scuttling in from Missouri
and we are strangers again.

REPLAY

Behind us the heavy weight of habit.
Light and dark's daily play. Inchoate
sadnesses in mind's weather.

We had become students of water.
Humor, our lusts
softening into love. Then something else.

The ferocious greens of storm
overtook us.
And the days found madness.

A look in the eyes. In the surly clouds.
The possibility of hope lay lost
and removed from our diminished shares.

The history of things
had become a story
of the sad.

We knew we traveled Express.
There would be no stop at the Happy Isles.
And we could come only so far.

Looking for something perfect
and serene.
We never found it.

All morning I tried to listen
to time, a steady wind, the river
at my side now unperformed.

BOOK FIVE

Strange Fruit

Time was. Time was.
White robes like moonlight
In the sweetgum dark.
Unbucked that one then
and him squealing bloody Jesus
as we cut it off.

Robert Hayden, "Night, Death, Mississippi"

From the beginning
angry auroral winds
raked the arboreal ferns
and tore at Cairo's Pliocene shore.
Blue, grey, and marine
green waves ruffling beneath
clouds of primordial dust, rain
long before the river ran.
An ancient history you tuned out
by turning on Dylan
and "The Times They Are a-Changin'"
under a corrugated roof
at Cairo years ago.
            There
where Princess Shoshanna's vane
was looking for another weather.
The late summer climate of a republic.

Stock of its founding charisms nearly exhausted.
After accumulating indulgences, its credit shot.
You switched stations and said
voices that should call us back
do not. Outdoors we ate pork barbecue, drank
sun tea. Listened to a mockingbird.
In the kitchen a woman was singing
Get up Jesus because . . . .
Well, there's a long day ahead.
Because a story
was looking for an end.
And behind the fat magnolias and urban sumac
a wildness kept watch.
                              All things
return to chaos you said. *It's a law.*
You'd been listening to the old man's
white-caned voice, hoarse from silence.
And asked *if westward the course of empire*
takes its way
why are we still going south?
                              Old black men
in animation, slow grey statues
ruined by sweat and rain
fingered their Orange Crushes.
Asking the price of an RC Cola.
Each man knowing more
than the world knows:
anything good that happens
counts against you later.
Bottleneck drone on a diddley bow
under the porch. Uneasy twilight
peopled with echoes
from fields, the cabbage patches. The tarpapered

slave shacks now whitewashed, fitted out in calico.
Today, 104 degrees, 93% humidity.
Our docent said "this is where the servants lived.
In cool shade on the porches."

                    Somnolent towns
backing up to reticent woods. Roadside mullein
and chicory. Pokeberry fencing fence rows.
Cricket singsong. Rasping cicadas.
We toured Colonel MacDougal's grand place.
Drove into Campbellsville. You thought
it looked like Holy Week.
Streets lined with boot-clad men
in white ceremonials. The Grand Wizard
just over from Alabama. His red Chevy pickup
angle-parked on the courthouse square.
Handshake, wink. Nod and ring.
Penitentes of a lost hope, their patience tried.
An older, wider salvation
unavailing.

                Princess Shoshanna owns these
deep woods darkening the road to Port Gibson.
Trestle and track on the way stare down. The water
bug-green.

            In the telling there will be
a white woman on the other side of a screen door.
And the black man will be beaten
and beaten again.
He will begin his mock trial in a Klan
square-dance barn.
Someone always has hounds, a gun.
Whiskey at the deckled edges
though this has been forbidden.
Women, children in the far background
for their own good.

Hot coffee. Arcs of
light. Flashlights and lanterns.
They are playing with his manhood
cracking jokes, taking its length
before slicing. To stuff in his mouth.
And two black fingers for pickling.
For the counter at the store, next to the register.
A voice taps a cane, says
theys do these things in the greenwood
what will they do in the dry.

                                Next day's sun
scents the air for green flies:
the dangle of strange fruit swinging
from a trestle . . . a mail train from Jackson
hurrying by.

                Hurries by where a billboard rises
—Princess Shoshanna, Madame Cecile offering
salves for hurts. Fortunes told.
Franchises are available.

                       From his kingdom
I watch Rufus grown old. Cherishing phantom
house and home. Guarding what no longer exists.
Evening turns in early now. And his days of endless
summers—we are what our memories are.

Time at the Mouth of the Arkansas

Arriving at the old river de Soto crossed
another river enters, a crooked road
out of the brindled West.
The gaping mouth of the Arkansas
vengeful—disrobing blood red
in evening light. A river shouting to
hapless travelers
stories of gold, the story of fur
carried by canoes, bateaux
though no two stories are ever quite the same.
De Soto tramping into
cool, foggy air.
Marquette dead. And Jolliet turning back
from the western, Spanish shore.
La Salle stopping close-by
in mist too heavy to see
and claiming everywhere
for France. You and I came this way before
but Cibola's Seven Cities
remained lost in their legends for us.
Night rhyme of crickets
jamming on an empty trail, if only for the stars.
The sky turned on its side, ready to empty its contents.

Black trees ahead
in the gloom of a dark wood.
Ground fog shrouding
wild pecan groves.
Morning sunshine, crows in the walnut trees chanting
receivables, the uncovered debts.
A calculus from old cotton futures
revealed in the stubble of the forgiving delta
fluvial. In larger fields John Deere
now picks the cotton. The fields no longer plowed
and the small farms gone. Monster machines
compacting the soil.
Brahman cattle mosey.
The Baptist dead nearby weather in
cemeteries, their churches worn.
Three in a congregation will opt for
salvation during altar call in one.
At the hamlets poor farmers sit on long
sagging porches.
Mice and Gypsy children
from the wandering caravans are safe again.
A Mormon marker tells how far
the lost tribes of Israel reached
into this fleeced paradise.
Prophets and apostles still preach
in local churches. Princess Shoshanna
has taken Universal Life holy orders.
Receives the ministerial
tax exemption.
Does local drive-by
marriages. The third and fourth for free.
Preaches the Apocalypse.
Holds the revealing seals, whatever they may be
—close.
A couple maybe in their seventies
walk on the levee holding hands.
They pick up a stick
to beat a dog.

The white miasma ahead
is river mist, river heat
where Pierre Laclède, having invented
Saint Louis, took on final
light-being under the sadness of fog.

Late Morning Prayer
in the Arkansas Delta

parties of Sunday birders
latitudinarians with
compasses
follow rumor
N by NW to where
the ivory bill last appeared

straining to hear
the bird's clarinet trill
for what was once
now lost

past empty crimped Coors
a party turning back
binoculars and cameras
hung like scapulars

and filing out near
the somnolence of noon
to a continuous circadian hymn
a powerboat
whang, whang, whang
follows them from the bayou

Delta Oracle

Madame Cecile

Palms · Tea leaves · Horoscopes

Destiny Read & Interpreted
(Dialogues with the eternal)

I am Madame Cecile, the Oracle
my role anointed, your fortune told
as the moving finger traces
—my words come from afar

but just now, I say, I saw you take a cigarette—
or was it a drag on tea?

sweet potato futures, price of yellow pine
local real estate, this year's cotton
are mere accusations of detail

listen—you only saw me sip on air

but where is this far?

it lies beyond the dead in their transport
I speak of dreams from bygones
their broken images brought back from deepest chaos

you began somewhere
why the toque, a purple gown?

I'm not what you think
I am a vessel
turbaned, this gown is purple for a purpose
truth passes directly through my vision

I thought you were from around here
Greenville, maybe Port Gibson

you have the bias of country people
the truth I speak of
I find looking into light, past the silences
free of place or time, the lure of things deceitful

now tell me

we were not happy
my love was melancholic
and I was, I—

and you were you
a teller of stories
bearer of tales
the child within
never left you

well, I was despondent—
what you say, that's another matter
I want to know what everyone wants to know

how amorphous, this happiness you seek
your determination shows me the child you are
all happiness is aberrant
what story is there to tell when you're happy

but I will put my hand on this crystal eye
and look for the answer

—in a dream I saw sacred cattle in a grove
they were being sent to slaughter

were there bodies near?
an altar?
a place where you could attend
the sacrifice?

I was afraid
and lonely
a man was crying

dreams summon or send
in them everyone you see is you
you must try to harmonize whatever
you remember or do

I'm too tired to think
how can I act when lines to what I'm saying
are unclear?

every despair has a savage air
even if you step outside your shadow
you are caught between Rimbaud
and Baudelaire

—*you can leave your shadow*
but not what shadows you
I see you will come back at once
only not as you were but as you are

I want my past to change
how will I recognize what I become?

you will reach and stretch beyond this doom
while we look into your destiny
—but for better definition we must consult the runes

first do this . . .

I see aurochs and angels!
but happiness is the highest good
or so the philosophers say

happiness and pleasure are not the same
concentrate on feeling
think about now, what you eat
later study Husserl, Fichte on consciousness

now quick, the Fork points to icy runes

Wungo shows me your loneliness and your despair
anxiety, separation from a deity you must bear

Tyr shows conquest at great sacrifice
truth or justice will prevail at last

Ger shows cycles of business that affect you now
flood and drought pass you by

Providence will continue for a little while
to move the Fork

yet how can I tell
what the Fork knows—

can this wound ever heal?
I'd like to sing for myself again
not in some narrow room
a place reserved for tomorrow

do you know the stories done in different voices
—are you familiar with minstrelsy?
life is funny, its ill-proportions comic
days and nights pass like jokes
hidden in dreams, their vatic songs

well, once I swore a man was Nietzsche
—in top hat, wearing spats
he was waving from a rumble seat, hat in hand
the abyss, he was saying, is on tour <u>B</u>

his last men, in an open car, were singing
"we have invented happiness"

now hear
I tell all who dream of happiness
send postcards to your future
only the important things put down
they will be read in your past

—but this serious work is arduous
what will it be worth to you?
I aged a hundred years—
this happened within an hour . . .

— — —

I imagine endless summers
their protracted, unbroken heat
favor prophetic narcissisms
you find here in the music—
in guitar riffs, the badgering of basses.

Squinting at the future one sometimes
finds the things that work
and mostly things that don't.

And at times you look back
to look ahead—well, to catch
a surfacing fault in time
and save yourself from some disgrace.

Apotheosis of Elvis

I

Of course Elvis lives.
Against backwater currents
a colossus astride the river:
his sneer, thrusting pelvis
(if you smile, where's
the threat). The whole world
stirring to its senses—
the voice of white gravel
with a black sound.
Col. Parker's boy
just an ordinary guy—
Dr Pepper for breakfast
like most Mississippians.
Ruffled cuffs and Corinthian
red satin pants
from Lansky's Memphis
where half the planet
once dressed.

II

The sped-up tempo, hoarse
guitar riff, the bass
slapped around: this gonna be good—
make your woman behave.
Subversion in little things:
strum and shimmy of the crotch
and shake of the southern ass.
Time's revelation turns to sass.

III

How could it have been otherwise.
A ring around the moon
vouchsafed only to Gladys
at parturition. Twin brother Jesse stillborn.
Elvis's birthright a double portion.
Then the chickens fried, a hog butchered.
Old Rte. 61 bouncing their truck
through kudzu from Tupelo to Memphis.
Lost years of vamped chords later
his public life now incarnational.
Drug-addled last years
and torments of the road (it's said
he was in all things like us
in his guile and weakness)—windows on his soul.

IV

All the sightings.
At Kalamazoo, Tunica, in Queens.
Healings at Baptist Hospital:
doctors and nurses dropping
to their knees. These will go on.
Maybe fewer with time. But count on it.
What else can it mean to believe.

Memphis on the Mind

Fat green widow on the river
sipping Gatorade, slipping from
your foundations. Accustomed
to the South's old mutterings.
African heat. Pigeons
the sole agitation. The city
of dry goods, Sun Records. Stax.
Guitar shops off Beale. The heartland
flyway. Buzzards. Long thermals
lofting their sky cruises. The nervous
sidelong glance for rot. Evening air
thick with insects and bugs.
Lassitudes after succinct meditations.
Quick sex. The blues. Well, Mr. Handy
we have met.
                    Bluff City limits
without a metaphysics
but three climates: two
with their own kings.
Crows leaning on one wing
gasping for air.
A woman shaking her finger
in West Memphis, Helena—
they'll slit your throat.

The Chickasaw Bluffs crumbling.
Your cobbled cotton landing
braked by Mud Island. The factors
and bales gone.
                    Lansky's sequined velvets
remembered. Pink. Purple. Turquoise.
Ladybug dare and clowning.
Part in-your-face.
                    Soulsville.
Nomadic Blacks from the hinterland
drawn to your flame. Cleotha.
The late B.B. King praying out loud.
"Green Onions" and Booker T.
At Graceland
Swedes, Germans, the Japanese
venerate the empty, brass-plated
tomb.
            A bullet's trajectory
in the arc of a blue-green laser
to the Lorraine Motel. There—
such things men will do
for a day's pay. Afternoons now
and women with orange plastic scarves.
In their pink rollers make ready for
tomorrow at The Holiness Church
of Sinners Redeemed in Blood
of the Lamb.
                    Ah, Memphis—
wise to dress in the winter mode.
A freezing rain, the shrill winds
blowing down from Hudson Bay.
Your days of noon birds overhead
a steady bass beat
primal and radical.
Everything else sold
or packed away. Time
already baled and wired ahead.
Feathers retreating.
Flood waters soon on the way.

Echoes from the Red River

I leave Memphis in the morning
looking for something
like a purpose
and find the Red River.
Months earlier it had
had a change of mind
wheeling in from the West and feeling
for a mouth.
It now exhibits illuminated passages
straight out of early winter
hours, the small towns waiting to be
named by God.

Show curtains whisking open
to the movie's summer cool—
the dawn, set to music, rising to a distant light.
Along the river headlands
a dusty stage for local stars.
And dreams of old divinities
on horseback, their mortal crises
to become an epic
slipped into Saturday matinees.

With Wayne and Clift
two tensions coming together, and a moral tale
for once got almost right.
Passion for range, a continent, the West
completing itself with the necessary
surfeit of solitude. Reaching an end
corrupted by an ending.

On leave from the humid deciduous
of the Mississippi
we tried to enter their story one summer
in the pale Oklahoma light
Coronado turned from.

We climbed down into its bed, touching
where the Red River lay, more breath
than water. Imagined cattle drives
on the Chisholm Trail, the railroad
no closer today, and found open sky.
Scurry of the black wind of Kansas
and a High Plains silt blowing in
to powder local poplars.

Listen—hoofbeats. A silver-dazzled bridle.
Things won or lost
flash by for our review.
Things intangible like memory
of a bracelet's story
or real like love—
chorded riffs recorded on a burled guitar.
Aren't we what our memories are?

This morning silent again.
A lone skiff oared on the river's glass.
From where does this huge water
come? Its sinewy evasions
gliding toward epic waters.

The river since has changed its course.

VICKSBURG

The Father of Waters again goes
unvexed to the sea. President Lincoln

Helmeted Athena, eyes hand-shaded
surveying dire Ilium
from the many-templed hill
reads the portent of war arriving
in drifts, the clouds large as continents
accompanied by preternatural force
Grant, his seven wounds mending
seeming at a loss what to do next
doing what he did best
without umbrage
believing in what he did

a new tenor of war deepening
gothic lines of war's architecture
daily crenellated sheets of fire
on an improvisational note:
a forty-day siege
and biblically bad weather
the bluffside tunneled with caves
a river and desert trading places
the cannonade
repeated like a temptation
then returned to as if by custom

ruin scented with late spring
nights of bayberry, lilac
early summer hickory
the long Corinthian smokestacks
of steamers, columns belching black
into the muzzle flash of falling stars
over colonnaded houses on the bluff
night river flare in the Palladian glass
and a young city garrisoned

awakening
to its old age to gnaw on defeat
and tasting of mule and rat
everywhere scabies, dysentery, death
sphincter of war's cloaca
sulfuring the downwind
for the Fourth of July
and women at the shattered windows crying

city of aftermath, graves, granite
markers, broken architraves
a city like Troy, pacified by intimacy
of battle, now foraging for a new history:
what to do with war
a war that has never really ended
—victory, defeat
what to remember, forget.

SHILOH

I sit under white oaks
old as the soldiers
they shade
their shadow
shadows no tree makes

—lovers drawn late to war
rendezvous with twilight
trysting in dew
devotion to maneuver
a display of coquetry

in the harsh falling out
of battle, loud arguments
running on until oaks alone
standing guard
bivouac with birds

men in springtime, the young
man I look for, their lives
and bodies, his tight grin
surrendered
to sky, the still moist grass

—spectral soldiers, one
an ancestor, falling in for
formation
to rise as a body
on a formal field of crosses

in love again, their company
each other
among battalions, regiments
fallen silent, and entrenched now
beyond the arguments.

Acorn from Oak Alley Plantation

for Aline Johnson

When you first walk up
the oak-canopied lane
you feel there is much
to be said for shade: a line
of families from the shadows
has already marched out
to bury their dead, passing
seasons of architecture

a house leaning on columns
adequate for their burdens
though not for pox of war
the live oaks standing
like cadets at drill
an inheritance settling into tourist
museum, country park folly

in old photographs
the slave shacks fieldside
on stilted perches
and poultry scratch yards beneath
left as memories of negative spaces
awaiting demolition

at the levee a plantation store
swallowed
whole by the river
pecan grove, sugarcane fields
vanished
generations of boyhood secrets
the edgy clarity of youth
erased
with the *garçonnières*
all the boys grown
and gone
the young sent off to war

Aline, you know already the acorn
you took with you
and planted at Métairie
is now on its way to immensity
and has taken root beyond the private
arguments of any particular place
its past like the sun running from time
a past looking for the shade of its shadows.

Folding the Rain
on the Delta Queen

Heaving against currents
the fire-red paddle wheel
washed a broad aft. The jazz bar
window etched to splendor light
and a night field of stars.
We're going wherever this goes
I had said.

Pushing beyond Baton Rouge
St. Francisville   Natchez.
A whisper cruising on water
beneath incoherent clouds.
Vicksburg   Memphis.

We were still together then.

Taking broad oxbow bends—
we plowed through calm, steady rain.
Crystal shudder at table. Reverse
of the Pittman's bold downstroke.
Hull twist, chandelier tinkle.
A man pushed back his chair and said
Beauregard wasn't a very good general
you know. Overrated. Still is.

Is good at war the same as bad at war?

At the tying-up below Houmas Plantation
a landing stage reached for the river
—our feet no longer feeling the pivot
toward levee, allée, house.
The calliope's muted Donizetti
insisting we had arrived.
All the while you had hidden out
from the Age of Aquarius.

After furious nights of denial
a fog of madness had settled in.
Our destination seemed to be
a pentecostal place
imperceptible just yet.
But voices everywhere.
Some that spoke to you.

You listened to Bruckner
from Rosalie to Longwood
on an invisible, golden wire.
Heard largo movements of the waves.
Starboard—saw birds Audubon painted
skiing on lagoon glass.

In the red velvet parlor
Madame Cecile sat over her crystal.
She said *all I see is woe.*
In my work I seldom smile.
Fleeing bingo, euchre we walked
the texas deck. Watched nut-brown water
part for our cargo.

A gentle cradle of the packet
rocking cabin and stateroom
through smoke-windowed summer.
A water clock ticking the seconds
before you felt you had to leave. Forever.
A measure of urgency
I think you took to wherever you went.

Earlier we had stood at river edge
watching rain stipple water.
We saw a landing running into the past.
I had thought of time
only as duration. Like a sunset. Isn't loss
always about time? Time's refusal.
Time running out.

BESSIE SMITH

I hate to see the evening sun go down.

You're leaning on my bar. With a haze
of grainy monotone, the film I'm watching you in
is never quite black and white.

A place too nice for juke-joint ramble.
Glasses *ching-ching*. Gold glinting
on marine shellac. No more field
hollers. Seamless ebony out of
pure black. A voice from between
your legs. That heavy. Smoke and fun.

*Hold that engine, let sweet mama get on board
'cos my home ain't here, it's a long way down the road.*

Sad like evening dew.
Blue smoke rings curling in the light. Dancing
the black bottom. Monkey hunch.
The shimmy. So many years
of raunch. Such swine men are.
Slack, bruised flesh. The heat.
Sugar and honey. The Memphis pulse.
Fist of the heart. A red silk dress.

Two things I don't understand . . .

afternoon weather inside—and the heat's
prostration. Well-fingered curls
in the pubic patches. Black cocks risen
to a magnitude.

I'm wild about that thing.
You make my ding a ling.

Such swine men are.
That diamond smile. A little gin.
Some fun. A short stutter and step.
Then off to Mobile.
Your opal, the money with it. Gone.

Backwater blues done caused me to pack my things and go . . .

You can live only so long
up and down Rte. 61.
What does an unruly girl do?
Cornbread's done. The pigs feet too.
Catch that train to Memphis.
People want to sell you like a mule.
And men don't change.

O watch out for that biscuit truck!
Yes, I said that cracker truck!

Trouble, trouble, I've had it all my days.
It seems like trouble is going to follow me to my grave.

You have to go.
A long line follows.
The green, fat land. Arrow of the sun.
Past catfish fries. Creeper.
Shotgun shacks. Life's tumbledown.
After the gravy. All the grief.
The reckless fun.

Delta Wedding

Negotiating purple night
over dusty green terrain
a groaning board for nutrias
then a turn lane
past the crack house

the couple speeding, their skeletal
language of love already engraved
in cabin entertainments, strobe-lit by
lantern lightning in the west
fireworks shooting cobalt
cochineal, cadmium, chrome
the grump of tuba, other bass follow
each a party to the night's detailed specifics
guests dressed to match
and scrutiny of the amber light
at the courthouse square
hyped as well with repetitive cautions—
jars of white lightning, rummed Cokes
a purely functional cake knife
all other blades
to be left at the church door

the couple swaying in
under red light, holler and call traded like
pork bellies at bidding time, a feeling
like an epoch waiting, deferred until
the right epic comes along

this is the Delta, a goat
noodling the hog in a yellow pickup
and three cars
fender-bent at the four-way stop.
Down the road is unclear
though night returns the dangerous world to
the day star's morning blue.

DUSTING THE BROOM: DELTA BLUES

You joke around all night, Robert Johnson.
You know you do.
Feeling for your shoes.
Buttoning your coat.
Tonight you're singing for us
again about another man's wife.
Howlin' Wolf will soon be coming through.
He'll match you two to one.
Robert Johnson, worry your
blues, the fished-out ponds.
Beg your bed and board.
Follow the afterglow of that train
to the midnight moan.
Leave those aches back
in Helena, Jackson.
Catch that Gulfport Island Road.
Hello, Ship Island. You still there?
Danger takes to the dark—Robert Johnson.
You said so. When the crossroad
stops, you can run faster than a Terraplane.
No use to holler for Willie Brown.
Darkness, they will say, is taking hold.

A Modular House Traveling South on Rte. 61

The wide-bodied sequence of rooms
looking for a perspective, a place
to anchor, and homesick for permanence

Port Gibson's rush-hour traffic
shoulder swerving

to let a room for ferns
dropping their leaves
for no reason at all

squeeze by, wrapped like a gift
in plastics fluttering

another room where arguments
might end in moonlight shade
finessed by body arts

with luck a room for silence
apart from evening's communion
in blue light solitude

or where a couple might watch a video
together of the river at full flood

portico, columns of a planter's house
if added
announcing final destination, an arrival

ceremonious, almost civic like Lee in marble
the view broad
fronting here on time's unhurried road.

Shorty Sam's Car Graveyard: an inventory

Chromed accounts of internal combustion
in the long rear view, behind the Johnson grass
and a rusty, corrugated fence on the road to Monroe

your grandfather's Rocket 88
an Oldsmobile from the Silver Age of Ike
interned behind a patch of weeds

a 1947 bottle-green long-stroke
flathead Lincoln Continental
the reward after five years for insider trading

its broken grille, the baroque smile
in perpetual adoration

from the mechanic's shack
clang and bang of infernal forces (a broadcast of
Shostakovich's Fifth, the mechanical procession
from Vulcan's bench, Makksim conducting?)

off to one side, five urinal Edsels
barged from across the river

shared at LSU by two co-eds
a Henry J *perdu* laid out on its back
weathered to *marron glacé*

1950 Kaisers paired, rebels of lost causes
one still in coffin grey, a Frazer hatchback
on the verge

if the universe inclines occasionally to life
life inclines quickly to details

a '57 Plymouth in hot boudin, with the craquelure
of netted casket veils, and rouged Chevrolets
—one that has seen the USA with Dinah Shore

pungent motor oil volatiles leaking from oil pans
into the universe, the universe taking a back-charge

mummified Windsors, Saratogas, a Chrysler
Town & Country, blond, mapled woods
an upscale New Yorker, a sister with chromed airs

its green luminescent steering wheel
Egyptian moderne speedo detailed
   blue > green > orange > red

all baleen and ballast with eight ventiports
the postmaster's midnight-blue Roadmaster
mounted on blocks, returning to its elements

two demure Crosleys in Cherokee red
that drove every winter
to Frank Lloyd Wright's desert Taliesin

a military-olive Lincoln Zephyr
once bore the hanging circuit judge
trans-leaf sprung, at rest in funeral parlor pallor

an engineer's smooth-cut
emerald 1949 Cadillac parked on gravel
Hydra-Matic takeoff, forward in four gears
last incarnation before the Norden bombsights

two Fords, boy and girl: a '49 Tudor
and a '50 chrome yellow pickup
now surpassing V-8 rapture together

if the planet inclines
to life, life inclines to decay, American
exceptionalism, vast US cast iron

Studebaker's Dictator and President
(what were they thinking in South Bend?)
fenders, running boards missing

a sky-blue Champion coupe, avant-garde
in the twinkle of Loewy starlight

the *sine qua non*—a teardrop Packard
with an in-line eight unable to survive the '40s
sadness at the end of great metal

meiosis leading to metastasis
the doctor's step-down Hudson
definitely not in remission
blister, chancre, canker, cancer
rust

(unmistakable bee buzz
somewhere—is that the Carters singing?)

one 1946 Nash Ambassador with
postwar bumpers of unidentified lumber
a priest's car intoning
clerical conundrums, graveside temporalities
soon to be swept by floodwaters.

Near the double cattle-gate entry
among America's nostalgic desiderata
a Ford's Philco still plays
Will you miss me, miss me, miss me . . . when I'm gone?

Book Six

CATCHING MASS
AT ST. FRANCISVILLE, LA

At the landing a back-thrust harrumphing
of the S.S. *Credence*. I slip into the space
between a pickup and a BMW. The Big Bopper
out of the past singing "Chantilly Lace" from
someone's radio. Moans of a crated heifer
on the truck. I lower my window, say
hope you're not
going to a sacrifice.
                              She's sure on her way
to a barbecue. The ferryman
stands over me, nursing on a stogy
Well, well. You be lookin' for the river
pure, the water of life, clear as
crystal. Yes sir, there be no night there.
Now that'll be two dollar.
No blink from his black, sacerdotal eyes.
He climbs to the cab, swings the tow and
connects with the car barge.
                              I imagine
far beyond the landing on the other side—
the Easter story there, those chanted Latin
syllables, a habit of hope—all pull me to
the approaching fixed point
of this now-turned world.
Yes, I know the evidence is not good.
Think of Hume, his take on all that.

But in the long reach of nature's odds
an intractable culture, the immovable tribe
—the fallenness of everything, the world
is more beautiful than it needs to be.
And the infinite that is everywhere
feels near.
             So I join a party of searchers
in the company of seekers. Where I'm headed—
I believe we're that close. And I continue on.
Earth in my veins. Details to follow.
But no cigar. Not yet.

Night Voices

Once you had liked the trim green of the north.
A landscape without dust. What you looked for
you found purer at the river's upper reaches.
In frosted marshes, the snowfields
where the river begins. Although the old Nordic
divinities of sun and creation were nowhere
to be seen.
                    But we had drifted far to the south
where our days began with an edge.
With Sunday's tedium and the comics
and Madame Cecile's Sunday morning column
of fortunes and runes. And back-page showboat ads
for dramas with mad domestic scenes.
Paul Bunyan and his kindly Blue Ox
never roved this far. From our nomadic abodes
we had watched what was passing
passing beyond our ken.
                    After three grunts
on the calliope, Capt. Billy stood at the gangplank.
And Madame Cecile turned her mind
to destiny. In the melodrama of the inevitable
onboard, almost all will suffer. All will die.
So what we know and what we believe
need not be different stories after all.

A wash of lights colored the night clouds
white, red, blue. Next to us the *Casino Royal*
had tied up, rocking with the current. Just as
America was looking for the right slot, a trump
card, its new pastime. And quickly remembered—
somebody who loves you
has your number.
                        There were shadows here
from the past. Rogation Days that went unobserved.
Crudities of the West that affronted Lee. Vicksburg then
was on its own. And Grant as was his wont had taken
the high ground when he came through.
                                        You had played
"Profoundly Blue." Remembered Muddy Waters
said the blues had a baby hereabouts.
A troubadour from Tupelo barging upriver
taking three chords at a time with backbeats.
So we listened to "Blue Suede Shoes," "Heartbreak Hotel"
—although the music wouldn't dance.
We sang along with "Blueberry Hill."
                                    The last
of the century now lay on its side, shattered for me.
I continued to wander the river up and down
open to prevenient grace and looking for a place
to settle in. I couldn't go back to an office.
Face the moving horizon of accusing numbers.
Hedge commodities to enrich rich bankers. And so
for four hundred miles
I retraced the Natchez Trace.
                                Listening to talk radio
and Princess Shoshanna's utterances to the nation.
Return to the gold standard.
Eliminate the income tax.
Balance the budget.
Keep guns legal. Protect the right
to stand your ground. Pack heat at 7-Eleven.
Open carry in church.

                    The iron-latticed windows
on the motel where I stop say
stay inside. I awaken to a mirror.
Baton Rouge's sleepless refineries firing carmine light.
I remember and hold on to what I hold on to.
You long ago forgot an earring when you left
before that dawn. I'm still drawn to things that get lost.
Easily broken. And define some measure of us
for us as we become what we remember.
                                    The world's familiar
has moved. Only the walls are left. *Tabula rasa*, yes.
There's a river—not the one de Soto found.
And Spain's dominion is reclaiming its voice.
Every day I practice Spanish. And taking leave
of time's vernacular, I recognize almost nothing
except the white cane tapping its slow code.
¿Señor, por favor, cómo terminará todo esto?
                                    I hear
you have found a new life amid the old disorders. Mercy
in the meds. Extracts of nightshade. You once said
voices that should have called us back
did not. Will they ever? When Princess Shoshanna
stares through the parting clouds, maybe we will reappear
at last undisguised in our original dust.
                                    Indian summer—
fall spreads over water seen through lenses of the river optics.
Earth's fast-turning kaleidoscope
settling on yellows, oranges, reds.
In the morning I revisit an old scene.
Choppering above Pilottown, the pilot lost
in radio static. Early light opens over
the Head of Passes. There are clear sea-lanes.
Skimming low we hover above
a sedimentary trail of earth's mementos.
With field glasses I watch the river's grand flotsam—
a round-screen Zenith console, porch pillars. The door to
someone's imperiled keep.

                  The past collecting its valuables
and indifferent to now and us. Leaving behind meth-tinged
neighborhoods. Thirteen-year-olds on foot
shopping for elixirs at dusk. In hoods and baggy
pants so undercover won't notice.
With a wide turn onto Main Street
of America's lower reaches, the Johnson grass
Control Officer points his weed-green truck
into the traffic, lights out. Now looking for
Palmer amaranth.
                     Far off
the long-telegraphed taps of a white cane and a voice saying
history be all wrongs.
                    When you left you said
you would not come again as a flower.
A lotus floating back on black-green water.
But in a flaking pier glass, a spectre at arm's length.
And by then we shall have become sad Vergilian ghosts.
Shades in a long-forgotten story.

MUSIC ON THE LOWER MISSISSIPPI: A DIRGE

We had watched light on the water dancing.

For months on end the river's lulling savor of silt.
Ammonia. Summer guilt. The past passing through

in the history of things, incidentals in the life
we shared.

But you said, *people are ruined by a story*
Gatsby and his shirts, the duke and his bride
America and the politics of apple pie.

Whichever, from the brown Missouri south
traffic on the river to its mouth
runs wry
with American commerce.

Is it just here, or the world I hear?
You want to know, *can one put down—*
put down roots on water?

Monsignor sat at the window
playing Patience. The Queen of Hearts.
A whirling black LP—

"Poor Children's Begging Song."
"The Drunken Song."

Wasn't this the country we were looking for?

You listen to the call-ins. The nation sounds bloodied.
There's something dark in the DNA.
(Though we found our acre and the house we needed.)

And the land still felt easy on the American plan.
Daniel Boone playing Father Moses
showed which way
with his sly Quaker odyssey.

A land exempt from history in the East.
Destiny waiting like greed, breathless in the West.
A city set on a hill.

Here they say—with that innocent grin
history need not apply.

So we try checking in again.

The farther stars had sent a chill. Wounded
brass arrayed in disarray. Music
for a dance. Or two. Custer's Last Stand.
The Teapot Dome. Or for a simulacrum. One will do.

Coyotes now howl at a sentry fire
throwing its glow like the sun.
Parsi light fires the night sky. Refinery glower
from Wood River to Port Sulphur. The old oil culture.

After intermezzo, in twos and threes
(you and I no longer dance past twelve)
we huddle instead in the shadows of the oboes.

Monsignor believed music, you can hear it
in the doleful cellos, is the rumor of forever.

Peering out the window he said
don't look now. Nodding to
moon and clouds, the hills' adagio, carefree
as the blooms.

Our landscape, he said, is not yet composed.
Harmonies hover 'round four notes
still to be used.

Talk radio had tuned in to the Apocalypse.
The angels of numbers and the numbers of angels
continuing their quarrel.

Music of our republic turns shrill.
There's a thinning in the reeds.
You spin the dial.

In this game the odds of winning are small.
Monsignor played his hand as best he could.

You say you believe in chance of late.
But there are no toll-free numbers left to call.

Except for accident. Or fate.

The horns uncrossed their feet, weighed in with bruit.

Mad, mad music. Those are the brasses
of the republic always at war. Louder, louder.
A band rounds the corner. They are tearing down
downtown.

We searched everywhere for the well-considered life.
In memories, the traffic of hustling trains, familiar stars.

There's only banging of conjugal MoPac cars.
We hear nothing that sounds like home.
Like acid and poof of spoiled tomato jars.

The great brass kettles summoned, drummed
atonement for notes long-ago denied.

You now follow nights to their source.
I fiddle all day with volume, sound.
There is music but we no longer dance.

Everyone, slipping their fevers, leaves
if only for winter. Better money.
Neglecting Indian remedies, the curdle of a Spanish
caudle. Now catching their breath, coughing
phlegm. The catarrh—from old Monsanto air.

But wait a minute!
This universe isn't fully created.

So, you've already caught the red-eye special out.

Then isn't *here* the same as *now*?
Aren't most of us looking for a canopy
of stars? A Chevy and an acre or two

a place at the end of a rainbow
path, off the Indian road?

Still, stars kept shifting. Our life together
over. We had submitted to the world's chaotic heart.

The half measures we took. And all addresses
lost. How easy to get things wrong.
Those black-clouded clues missed by us.

Some follow a GPS
to the courthouse square.
Waiting for the music to change.
But they're selling off Benjy's pasture there.

Like water I keep moving with the river.
Listen to the darker local stations wherever.

The lost republic of grace receding in the mirror.

Maybe that's the way people look for God
who look for God. Monsignor slapped down his queen.
Hearts trump diamonds. Still, part of it is
how you play, he said. He turned the record over.

Sarah! Come back! Come back, wherever you are!
It's our song.
I'd recognize it from anywhere.

Such vulgarities. The beaten drum.
Trombones in retreat. Their elegies.

Half the orchestra played capriccioso.

Aren't we often miscast by history?
Our lives disguised to us, we glimpse
ourselves only in someone else's story.

A yellow Camaro—windows down, with thumping
base, a grim-faced boy—thundered by.
Va-va-vroom. Vroooom. VROOM!

The music stopped. Monsignor said
don't count on being happy. It's a symphony
of farewells. This music wants to be
incomplete. But what's left unfinished
is seldom heard.

He slipped the albums back in their case and said
this is how it ends. Nothing ever seems finished
even though there's a beginning and an end.

I was unsure what the times were saying.
You were gone. The home, a house for sale.
But hope still shored up my faith. Open to
what's ahead I wanted to believe. In the green
light at the end of the dock. The river's blousy blues.

At Kellogg's Landing with Rufus I watched
the river passing and wondered what remaining magic
if any could bring time back and repair the world.

CARVILLE

Indian Camp Plantation Leprosarium

When you arrive
at the river road's turn-in
somebody at the address
already directs traffic
to history that has been here and left

fearful of its coded love
luck holds off the vegetable rot
furtive as armadillos
licking for fire ants
moss lacing live oak limbs
hands reaching from behind
pressed over your eyes—
surprise!

out of fear's lost diseases
its uncut pages of stories, small relics
like a watch peeling its silver, a lock
of hair, key to the future, a reliquary
of dreams, huddles of maggots and flies

life lived at subsistence, normal life
misplaced, dead-ended in dark magnificences
of oak here in night's irreducible
and another body settled into

with hand over heart
as if pledging love
love hardly possible
a finger pressing this way, that way
for white
as few lovers know
the turbulent, numb undertow

a blank world
once encrypted here for all to see
in flesh no longer yours.

Port Allen

At Refinery Row magical synergies
imitate the old divinities—serious
tasks of transmutation, a quiet alchemy.
Thermodynamics of a pagan god hovering
between Baton Rouge–Wood River
and illuminating cities at night
to dispel penumbras of our inner darknesses
the lonelinesses of empty squares
with Euphrates oil.
Exxon, Midhurst, Shell—still in their
white spheres, venting liquids, exuding
acrid volatiles.

In the fire lane a djinni is saying
Stop! Go no farther.
A voice understood by the guard
and checked through provisions
of a prism. There will be no fourth
fifth, or sixth dimensions.
Expect only ether, oils, and spirits
in shaded meanings of sense
refined to a viscosity. These mysterious
essences of power
like an outbreak of malevolence
have risen from earth
and grown into immensity.

An old man on his knees
rummages among used silences, old
noises, hose in hand. Metal
musics piping interconnectedness:
red > blue > green > yellow
coded and coda
Placid, Gulf, Scurlock.
Slippery extrusions coming
and going, alloy and polyvinyl
like implant and bypass.
Hiss from towering spiral
minarets, a Parsi jet
licks at interstices of day and night.
Incendiary designs of Persian carbon
and internal combustion in a race.
Hess Energy creating its own space.

In a motel I undress
and dress in gaudy light.
A pyre burning
in the bureau mirror: a scryer with
alembics asking
what had to die, decompose
to fossil or gas
so we can go.

Another Near Eastern deity with a name.
Lacking only transcendence
and using its tongue like a flame.

City of Obsequies

I followed the river again to its monument
the year after my father died. Years after our life
came apart. The songbirds had disappeared.
And the pelicans, cormorants muted their cries.
I hid out on highways. In a state of mind between
eternity and the future, looking for an escape
through gaps in stories the dead tell.
I reached the moon-washed city
waiting for me in a wide bed
naked.
        Sick, with a fever, I looked for
bitterroot. The air tropical and scented
with coffee, anise. Looked for Voodoo, the romp
of six histories weighting the past. Cajun
wails, a ballast of perils and D. L. Menard set free
on Toulouse. Dirge of "When the Saints Go Marching in"
at Preservation Hall. A cemetery stomp.
Feral cats scampering after phantasms
in the park. The pall of things to cover grieving
otherwise found only in fountain mist.

Silence never stayed long enough for
my future to ponder time. And what
a discriminating past reverences here—dead noon's
flit of angry cardinals, plastic daisies in Mason jars
set against marble tombs.

Already a remorseless
sun, its silent jackhammer vibes
approaching closer. Temple Sinai
on St. Charles, tent-white and feigning
desert's shimmer, opened its doors to breathe.
In Jackson Square bells chimed nine times.
Seersucker. Panama straws and rot of plantain.
A lonely, desolate girl weeping
where Ursuline crosses Rampart.
Bereavement's fog. Hurricane storms.
Moon silence whitewashing tombs
darkened by the Big Easy's failing memory
of preservation and fratricide.
Redemption now running to a good
martini at Galatoire's. A dinner run to Mosca's.
The world in case one forgets is a cornucopia
of perishables.
                    I can see I have followed
the life current of a river in shadows of grieving
because of you and the world you left.
I wanted to stay here only long enough
to suffer my father's ghost. After obsequies
behind the louvered light, floating dust motes
connected me to an ekphrastic spirit world.

Spiders blaspheming in a Vieux Carré window.
A trinity of flies heralding a new
theology: death perhaps no more
than a steady reign of disappearances.
The river running off to its mouth.
Ghosts drunk and throwing up
emerge from behind the levee. From Africa
it takes Voodoo spirits five hours.
One way.

Somewhere in the outlier world of the wild
a blind man taps his cane again.
Dear Mother, let me in. Let me in.
The dark, bent figure hard to tell in the darkness
from evening's subtle wiles.
My father dead. Rufus now. Their ashes waiting.
And you and I barely recognize the years
we once shared.
                    After 2,500 miles this is a river without
sign of any consoling structure.
And the city, ruled by moon and surrounded
with water, is prepared for me
after its run-ins with oblivion.
New Orleans *déracinée*.
Born of water, earth, and spirit, I stay.
Only the gods leave after an indecent
interval. To regain their innocence.

STORYVILLE: A SPORTING LIFE

They're gone now. Blue Book blue bloods.
Lulu Rich. Mittie Watt. Matrons in
shoulder boas, crinoline. Madams presiding
over the *Almanach de Gotha*
of the sporting flesh.
In back rooms, working women
of color, white girls, octoroons lined up
to serve male bidding, chance's choice.
Maud Franklin, Grace Bouchard, Viola Boss.
They knew the early flapper styles. Some
dressing as new brides. Convent schoolgirls.
A few with whips. At Mahogany Hall
the great staircase rose on the way
to finding yourself at eighteen. Or forty-five.
Mere visitation for some, one of the ephemeral
entr'actes. For others a meditation
or a defining moment. The remembered satin
sheets, ivory dildos. Cool skin
and the humid heat. Flounced tables
of rouge pots, French perfume in lucent vials.
Aromatic philtres for the lonely magic of need.
In someone's parlor Jelly Roll
doing "Professor at the Piano."
Louis, still a kid, in the back
hodding coal. "Pretty Baby" plinked out
in another parlor, pink in the red light.

Poker always a diversion for patrons downstairs.
These were love's lost novitiates
framed in lamplight and faceted sadnesses of night.
Bienville Street until 2 a.m.
receiving such honored guests
once recorded in visitors' books.
Babe Ruth. P. T. Barnum. Maybe a president or two
down on business. And my neighbor's grandfather
(he said). Others whooped it up at the Funky Butt.
Where else to go—it's hard to say. You could find
novelties, world-renowned specialties in backrooms
of the Black Terraplane. It was easy to get lost—
maps helped you find the way.

COMING OF THE RAIN

If the rain would only stop.
I duck inside the Fort.
A lady selling tickets remembers
just about everything.
Hard clouds low, arched. Farragut
at angles. Shipping his fleet
up-channel, still levee-less, riding
lower than today. Above Fort St. Philip
the shell trajectories branched like oaks.
From a redoubt made to be invincible
they must have thought
if only the rain would stop.
Cannon music heard sixty miles away
an acoustic shadow of war
now a headline in New Orleans.
And Fort Jackson's brickwork trenched:
once the symmetry of a severe geometry.
Everywhere the wadding wet.
Gunpowder turning to paste.
There was water up to here, she says.
In the gloom I could see a mere ration
of light left for shadows.

Farragut's marines with pinchers
in vanguard skiffs: cables across the river
cut. Thunder. Twice more
before the sun went out. She says
they never fought fair, everybody knows.
Our generals never stood a chance.
I survey the shop's souvenirs. Find no
reminiscences of the young sent off to war
by the old. No recordings of Rebel cries.
Throat-rattles of The Lost Campaign.
No candles for lost causes.
This morning I'm her only customer.
If the rain would only stop, she says.

Returning along the Atchafalaya

shadows of winter, amber fall
light, night immense here

if you were a ghost
in the house on the Teche
needing definition, a month
in New Orleans to take on
substance

the boat will take you a slow day
up-bayou to the Atchafalaya
a passage through raucous
Louisiana night
the earth waterlogged—earth burial
no longer to be trusted

the marble necropolises
remembering only time
and telling nothing of what you believed
or who you were

and when you return, if you should
come again by way of the Gulf
past the salt mines at Morgan City
whether as skeleton or ghost
or as a woman at the window crying

—if you believe you will return
think of how this southern sun
one of the stars with time on its hands
will touch you when you hurry
toward your own jagged ends
as memory, ghost, or skeleton

to stand in line, ticket in hand
as you try to reenter a former life
too late for love
and returning, if you ever do—refusing
to take your place in an album
where the past gathers on a table
and we are what we remember

at the bend
everything still wants out
de Soto's bones snagged on a towhead
John Law's investors, lost friendships
lights in a window at Christmas
whatever else you and I left behind

At the Sea Mouth

I watch fugitive lights like fireflies
above a black meadow of dark water
the ships loaded with Toyotas
Chinese tires treaded like Firestones
Rolexes from Shenzhen
Arabian oil and gas
and with heartland cargoes
of grain, ammonia, coal
lifting anchor and heading into the Gulf
beyond the rushes, reeds, the islands
where a continent runs out
and seabirds sit down on water
the wide river a vast enigma
at flood now
ladened with the daily quiddities
of those living close
to the American quick
and gathering its skies, landscape
livelihoods, the toxins and mistakes
burdens of the poor, their soft despairs
all the surfaces and identity of a land
all that we remember
and taking them back.

Some Reading Notes for
River Road: A Mississippiad

Plan of the Poem

River Road follows the north-to-south trajectory of the River itself. The major cities line up in geographical order along the way. The long anchor poems introducing each of the Books telescope and foreshadow the landscape of events lying ahead. But each of the anchor poems glances backward as well as forward to consider what has passed in light of the present, and where the past remains present and the future only hypothesis. Thus a strict geographical progress is not in the offing: the twists and turns like the River's own in its journey to the sea mouth.

Book One

"Theophany at Lake Itasca" A small glacial lake in the lake and marsh district of north central Minnesota, Lake Itasca was determined by Henry Schoolcraft, in 1832, to be the origin of the Mississippi River. Schoolcraft coined the name "Itasca" from *veritas* and *caput*, Latin words for truth and head (origin), apparently to sound like an Indian word, however ersatz.

"Keeper of the River" In 1837, a few years after graduation from West Point, Lt. Robert E. Lee in 1837 was ordered to Saint Louis as superintendent (keeper) of the Mississippi River to maintain safe navigation for the increasingly important steamboat traffic. As an Army engineer, he served in a capacity anticipating the subsequent creation of the US Army Corps of Engineers that now maintains, among other things, navigation on the River.

"Nauvoo Abandoned" After the murder of Joseph Smith and his brother Hyrum in 1844 in nearby Carthage, Illinois, most of the Mormons left the area of Nauvoo (Illinois) and began their historic overland trek to the West under the leadership of Brigham Young. The poem has been paraphrased from the prose of Thomas L. Kane's *The Mormons* (1850) and R. N. and J. K. Ostling's *Mormon America* (1999). The town of Nauvoo has since been considerably reconstructed.

"Lock and Dam #10" There is a series of twenty-seven locks and dams on the Upper Mississippi River, which facilitate navigation of river barge traffic. Lock #1 is located in southwestern Minnesota. Lock #27, the Chain of Rocks Lock, is located just north of Saint Louis. (Below this point, on the Lower Mississippi, adequate river depth for navigation can be maintained without employing a lock and dam system.) Lock and Dam #10 is located near Guttenberg, Iowa.

Book Two

"Sieur de La Salle" One of the earliest French explorers of the Mississippi River, La Salle traveled the River by canoe in 1669 and again in 1682, claiming the River and surrounding country for King Louis XIV and France, and named Louisiana for the king. In 1684, La Salle returned from France and sought the sea mouth of the River from the Gulf of Mexico.

He was ambushed and killed on this expedition (in 1687) by French claimants to an area in what is now East Texas.

"Monks Mound" Today, the mound, once central to Mound Indian (or "The Mississippian") Culture, has lost nearly two hundred feet of its original elevation to erosion—both natural and man-induced. Archeological artifacts found at the site link its culture arguably to the Late Mayan Era.

"Cherokee Removal" At the instigation of President Jackson and Congress, much of the Cherokee Nation was required to yield its land to white farmers and was forcibly resettled on reservation land in the Oklahoma Territory in 1838. The long trek westward, supervised by the US Army, continued through a harsh winter in which many died—the toll sometimes estimated at a third of the Nation. The Cherokee crossed the Mississippi River near Anna-Jonesboro (on the Illinois side) and just north of Cape Girardeau (on the Missouri side).

Book Three

"Père Marquette at Kaskaskia" Kaskaskia, now an island in the River owing to a flood and channel change in the nineteenth century, is located in southern Illinois. Kaskaskia became the capitol of the Illinois Territory, and was named capitol of the state when Illinois was admitted to the Union in 1818.

Père Marquette was a Jesuit missionary, born in Laon, France, in 1637. He founded Sault Ste. Marie (Michigan), and later, with Louis Jolliet, surveyed the Upper—and part of the Lower—Mississippi as far as the mouth of the Arkansas River, for France. He came to the New World primarily as a missionary and evangelized the entire area, stopping and resting at Kaskaskia in 1665. (See "Piasa Bird," below.)

"Lewis and Clark Striking Camp" The Corps of Discovery traveled overland from the Mississippi River to the Pacific Ocean in 1804 to discover, in part, what exactly had been purchased in the Louisiana Purchase of 1803. Some of the factual material in the poem is derived from Stephen E. Ambrose's *Lewis and Clark* and Thomas Schmidt's *The Lewis and Clark Trail*.

"Piasa Bird" The Piasa Bird is a pictograph on the Illinois bluff of the River near Grafton, Illinois, and just north of Saint Louis. The original image, seen by Père Marquette and perhaps related to the Mound culture to the south, was destroyed by quarrying, and a reproduction, to which wings have been added, has been drawn on the bluff nearby. The name is of late invention.

"St. Louis: at the Crossroads" Henry Conrad Brockmeyer, an immigrant and Hegelian, helped the city to understand its historical destiny. He founded the St. Louis Philosophical Society in 1866 to promote understanding of Hegel's philosophy and to examine the role of St. Louis in the westward progress of history.

Book Four

"Treaty of Paris" Signed in 1763, the Treaty of Paris ceded to the British control of French territory in North America from the east coast of North America to the Mississippi River. The French relinquished control of the River forts, including Fort de Chartres, which was soon discarded.

"Mile Zero" There are two beginning map-mileage markers on the River, one at the Head of Passes (Louisiana) and another at Cairo, Illinois, roughly beginning the measure of the River's length on both the Lower and Upper River.

Book Five

"Time at the Mouth of the Arkansas" Pierre Laclède, a French fur trader and founder of Saint Louis, Missouri, died on his boat near the mouth of the Arkansas River on June 20, 1778. It is believed he was buried "in the wilderness" nearby.

Book Six

"Music on the Lower Mississippi: a dirge" The reference to Daniel Boone as Moses is derived from George Caleb Bingham's painting *Daniel Boone Escorting Settlers through the Cumberland Gap* (1850–51). The painting was lithographed and widely distributed throughout the States, and the original is in the Washington University art gallery in Saint Louis.

The Monsignor plays Mahler's First, Third, and Ninth Symphonies. Mahler had immersed himself in Nietzsche's *The Gay Science* before writing the latter composition.

"Carville" Carville (Louisiana) was the site of the last leprosarium in the United States, which is now closed.

"Storyville: a sporting life" For some of the information in this poem, I am indebted to Eric A. Powell's "Tales from Storyville," found in *Archaeology* November/December 2002.

"Returning along the Atchafalaya" The Atchafalaya River is not a tributary of the Mississippi River, but it is a *dis*tributary, formed at the confluence of the Red and Mississippi Rivers. Its navigable channels funnel some of the Mississippi River current southwest past Morgan City, Louisiana, and into the Gulf of Mexico.

ACKNOWLEDGMENTS

I acknowledge with gratitude the publications in which some of these poems first appeared.

> *Arkansas Review*
> *Big Muddy*
> *Blue Unicorn*
> *Borderlands*
> *Chelsea*
> *Cimarron Review*
> *Crazyhorse*
> *Epoch*
> *Notre Dame Review*
> *Phoebe*
> *Poetry Northwest*
> *Prairie Schooner*
> *River Oak Review*
> *Salmagundi*
> *Shenandoah*
> *Slant*
> *Southern Poetry Review*
> *Tampa Review*
> *The Yalobusha Review*

Some of the previously published poems appeared in different forms and sometimes with different titles.

I also thank the editors and first readers for their kind acceptance of the poems for publication.

About the Author

River Road is Robert Bense's fourth published book of poetry. He and Sonya Lyons live in Sacramento, California, and Waterloo, Illinois.

Belle Fontaine Editions
robertbense.com

Garamond Premier Pro font 12/13 used in text

CPSIA information can be obtained
at www.ICGtesting.com
Printed in the USA
FSOW01n0925231116
27755FS